FROM THE LIBRARY OF

Faye Klahn

DECORATIVE
DESIGNS

Ex Libris

DECORATIVE DESIGNS

BY

GRAHAM RUST

OVER 100 IDEAS FOR PAINTED INTERIORS, FURNITURE,
AND DECORATED OBJECTS

A BULFINCH PRESS BOOK
LITTLE, BROWN AND COMPANY
BOSTON • NEW YORK • TORONTO • LONDON

First North American Edition

Second Printing, 1997

ISBN 0-8212-2329-1

Library of Congress Catalog Card Number 96-84781

Designed and produced by

Breslich & Foss Ltd.

Bulfinch Press is an imprint and trademark of Little, Brown and Company (Inc.)

Published simultaneously in Canada by Little, Brown & Company (Canada) Limited

Printed in Spain

CONTENTS

. . . . .

This book is dedicated in gratitude to the memory of
Sister Mary Bonaventure Lavan O.P.
1880–1968

INTRODUCTION

· · · · ·

In my previous book, *The Painted House,* I presented designs and ideas for the mural decoration of every room in an imaginary house. This book, *Decorative Designs,* has given me the opportunity to include designs for panels, screens, furniture and other objects sympathetic to these schemes. These designs, unlike murals, have the advantage of being portable, and need not be a permanent feature of any particular house. Many of the subjects on the following pages can be used in different ways. For example, the many "portraits" of houses which I have painted over the years were often used as the central motif in designs including the interests and pastimes of the owner of the property, but they can also be reproduced on ceramic plates, placemats, bookplates, letterheads and furniture, as shown here.

As my intention in this book was to be of use to both the professional and the amateur painter, the ideas presented require varying degrees of skill in their execution. Working on one of the less demanding projects – a bookplate, for example – may be a good way for a relative beginner to gain confidence before tackling a more complex design or working on a larger scale.

Painting on walls and ceilings can be very strenuous, and I am now fortunate to have an assistant to help me. Rui Paes has worked with me on several large murals as well as with the designs for the jewellery and objects in semi-precious stones shown in this book. I have also enlisted the help of painters, gilders, cabinet makers, jewellers and other craftsmen, without whom it would have been impossible to realize many of these designs. Finally I would like to thank Laura Wilson for her endless patience and invaluable help with the text and Nigel Partridge for his skill in making sense of the plethora of sketches and photographs to produce such a pleasing design for this book.

SCREENS

The screen has survived in many forms over the centuries. Although folding screens are perhaps used less today for the purpose of excluding draughts, they have never really gone out of fashion. The screens in this chapter could have several functions besides decoration: dividing off areas of a large space for specific functions such as dining, working or sleeping; giving extra privacy to a room that is overlooked; adding depth or light to a small or sunless room, and hiding empty fireplaces during the summer months.

*ABOVE: Sepia study of Cynthia's grotto which I painted on the Greek island of Delos. The goddess
Artemis is sometimes known as Cynthia because she was born on Mount Cynthus.*

o   o   o

RIGHT: A panelled screen showing a view of Cynthia's grotto. It is presented in a rococo cartouche above a
trompe l'oeil *dado rail with marbled inlays below it. A further* trompe l'oeil *addition is the lizard
climbing over the cartouche to inspect the picture.*

II

12

LEFT: Study of a red and yellow "parrot" tulip.

° ° °

RIGHT: I have chosen to paint three different types of tulip on this panelled screen. The sheer multitude of tulip forms and the colours that range from the brilliantly intense to the delicate and subtle make tulips fascinating flowers to draw and paint.

ABOVE: This design for the end wall of the dining room needed to incorporate features which would disguise a service door on the left-hand side.

This sketch shown opposite shows the design for one wall of a dining room painted for Mr and Mrs Alistair Robertson at the Quinta dos Frades in Gaia, Portugal. The two lemon trees in blue-and-white pots are painted to look as though they are sitting on a terrace outside the room. The lemon tree in a pot (RIGHT) used as a dummy board, could brighten up a dark corner or act as a barrier to indicate that certain rooms or parts of the house are inaccessible.

∘   ∘   ∘

RIGHT AND BELOW: Two studies for the lemon tree dummy board.

16

LEFT: Painted in grisaille, this pastoral scene of a satyr playing the flute to a nymph is taken from a terracotta relief by the eighteenth-century French sculptor Claude Michel Clodion.

CABINET OF
WATERCOLOURS
o o o o o

I have always been concerned to protect the paintings hanging in my studio from the strong natural light that pours in through the large window and skylight, and this cabinet (*opposite*) has proved an excellent way to do it. It can house twelve or more watercolour paintings, depending on size, and is based on an idea of the architect Sir John Soane, who employed folding sections of wood panelling to hide his collection of watercolours from direct sunlight.

The outsides of the doors are painted in *trompe l'oeil* so that, when closed, they resemble a marble relief panel. The cabinet is very simple to make, being constructed from ready-made doors, and it could easily be reproduced on a larger or smaller scale. It is essential that the cabinet be firmly fixed to the wall in order to compensate for the combined weight of the doors and paintings.

o o o

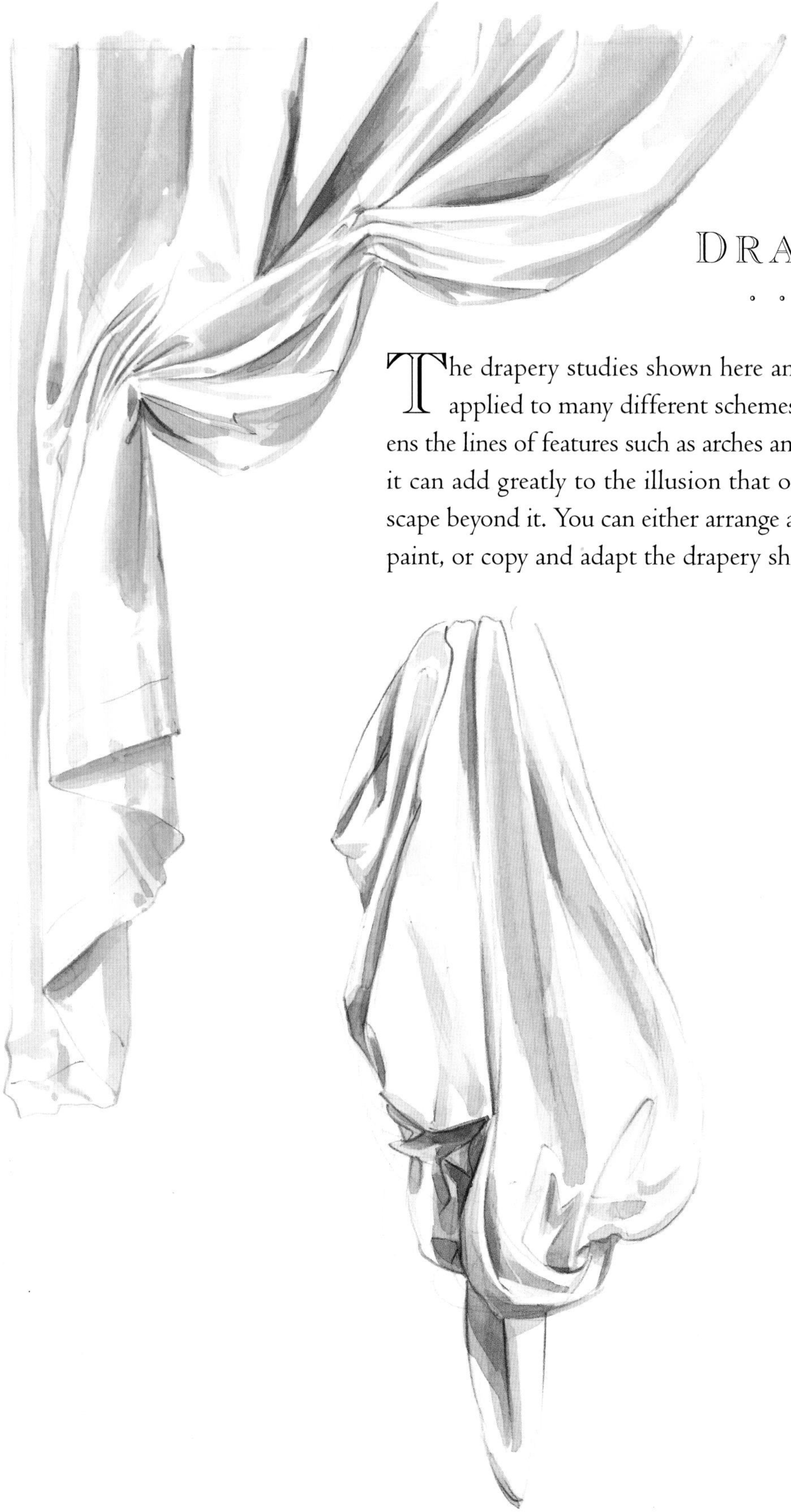

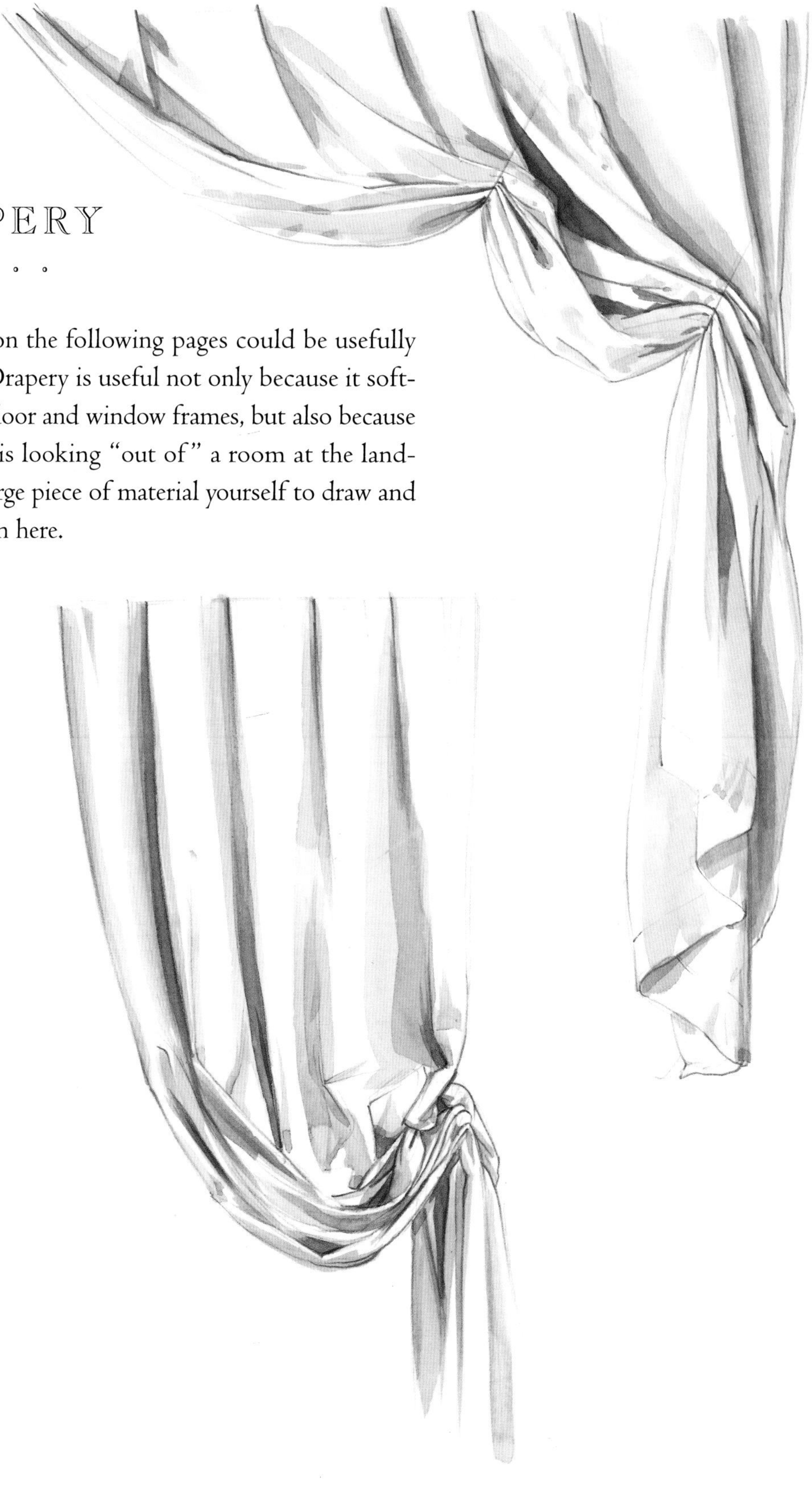

DRAPERY

. . . . .

The drapery studies shown here and on the following pages could be usefully applied to many different schemes. Drapery is useful not only because it softens the lines of features such as arches and door and window frames, but also because it can add greatly to the illusion that one is looking "out of" a room at the landscape beyond it. You can either arrange a large piece of material yourself to draw and paint, or copy and adapt the drapery shown here.

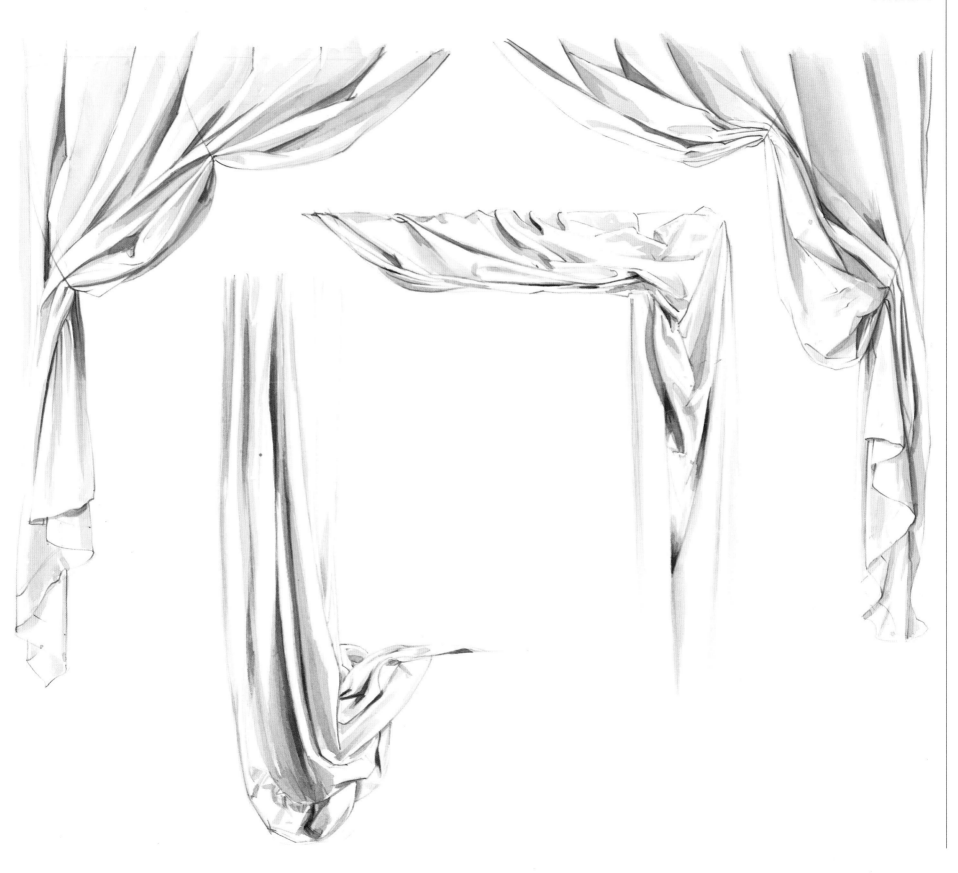

SWIMMING POOL MURAL

. . . . .

The mural shown below and opposite was painted for an indoor swimming pool owned by Lord and Lady Howard de Walden. The main wall on one side of the swimming pool was architecturally divided into four panels, and I used these and drapery in *trompe l'oeil* to give the impression of a colonnaded terrace looking out on a southern Spanish landscape.

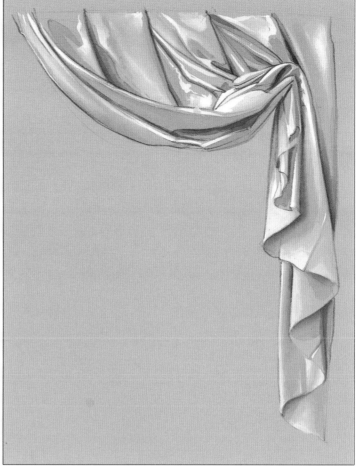

ABOVE: Two studies of drapery.

RIGHT: This sunny landscape, with drapery and a blue macaw painted in trompe l'oeil *inside a marbled architrave, would be useful as a false door or window to give an impression of open space inside a small house or flat, or to add brightness to a room that has little natural light. The landscape is a view at Paliokastritsa in Corfu.*

LEFT: Watercolour study of Paliokastritsa.

FIRESCREENS AND CHIMNEY BOARDS

· · · · ·

Many old houses retain their original fireplaces, and although nowadays fewer of them are used, particularly in bedrooms, even in the winter months, they still provide the room with a focal point. As well as enhancing a beautiful chimneypiece, firescreens and chimney boards serve the dual purpose of hiding an empty grate and preventing occasional falls of chimney dust and soot.

Firescreens and chimney boards should be lightweight and easily movable, so a canvas stretched across plywood or medium density fibreboard (MDF) is probably the best option. The firescreens shown here and on pages 25 and 26 are free-standing, and would therefore need a wooden support to the rear to keep them upright.

LEFT: These Chinese pots make a good subject for a firescreen because of their decorative appeal and simple shapes. Shape is a very important consideration in the choice of composition for a firescreen, because of the need to cut the image or images out of board. This factor should also influence your choice of subject — some flowers, for example, might look extremely delicate when painted but very odd when cut out of plywood in big, chunky shapes!

· · ·

OPPOSITE: Most dogs and cats like to claim a place in front of the fire, so the choice of a well-loved pet as a firescreen subject is particularly appropriate. Lindy, a pug, is shown here with her Turkish basket and a bowl of water.

26 *RIGHT: This firescreen, painted in monochrome, represents a terracotta sculpture, taken from a design by Clodion entitled* Poetry and Music. *The two* trompe l'oeil *kittens, playing hide and seek, give it extra interest and movement.*

ABOVE: The idea for this chimney board is taken from a work by Clodion, a frieze entitled The Triumph of Galatea, *and shows a merman blowing his conch, flanked by sea monsters and cherubs. I have included a line drawing of the moulding surrounding a fireplace around this board and those on the following pages, to put the designs in context.*

*ABOVE: I have given these Oriental pots an element of surprise by adding a lettuce-chewing
tortoise in the bottom left-hand corner. This chimney board would be suitable for a room opening
onto the garden.*

ABOVE: This chimney board, showing various painting tools and objets d'art, *would be well suited to a studio. The draped cloth, canvases, papers and wooden palette give plenty of scope for contrasting colours and textures.*

ABOVE: I made this study of an aloe when I was at Miletus, in Turkey.

*ABOVE: This chimneyboard was designed for the garden room of a house in Toronto. A toad crouches in
the shadows and a small snake is entwined amongst the leaves.*

ABOVE: It is sometimes fun to paint the unexpected and make people come back for a second look — the monkey shown here in a trompe l'oeil *fireplace has broken the vase, perhaps with the aid of the poker by her side, and is busily peeling the petals off one of the flowers as if she is saying to herself "he loves me, he loves me not."*

FURNITURE

This chapter includes various designs for pieces of furniture and their decoration. The designs range from a simple table, painted to look like marble, to a chessboard inlaid with precious stones. The decorative elements are interchangeable and could be applied to almost any piece in the house.

THE SUN AND MOON
COMMODES

. . . . .

34   This commode is one of a pair which I designed. It was made by the carpenter Maurice Hurst to be painted in *faux bois* by Jenni Lunan. The sun is surrounded by butterflies and the moon by moths. I felt that these motifs on the door panels were particularly appropriate for bedroom furniture.

. . .

ABOVE: Colour study for the sun panel.

THE SHELL GARDEN SEAT

· · · · ·

This garden seat was commissioned by *House & Garden* Magazine, who asked if I would collaborate with the Duchess of Devonshire in designing a bench for the Chatsworth Carpenters to produce for the Chelsea Flower Show. *House & Garden* wanted a seat which would be comfortable for two people but big enough for three. My love of shells and a late-seventeenth-century Venetian rococo chair provided the initial inspiration for my design. The final version was loosely based on a mid-eighteenth-century seat by Thomas Chippendale which also made use of shells. I decided on a grey-green painted finish because it is particularly sympathetic to garden foliage, but the seat can, of course, be painted in any colour you wish.

My intention was to make the seat reasonably comfortable, but it is intended primarily as a decorative feature for the enhancement of a garden or terrace, not as a purely functional piece of outdoor furniture.

BELOW: My drawings for the front and side elevation of the shell seat.

RIGHT: The finished seat, photographed on the roof terrace of my studio, against a background of black trellis.

HEADBOARDS
. . . . .

I first saw a painted headboard in the Ca' Rezzonico Museum in Venice. It was an eighteenth-century Italian piece in the form of a shell with a garland of flowers. As I sketched it, I realized that this idea would lend itself to any number of subjects, including the twelve that are shown in this chapter.

Any of these designs may be adapted to reflect personal tastes and interests. The headboards themselves may be cut out of block-board, plywood or MDF, and may be fixed either to the bed or to the wall behind it. Once the shape has been decided, it must be scaled up and cut out, then primed and painted with undercoat. You should then scale up and paint your chosen design on the board.

. . .

OPPOSITE: This simple panel, designed for a single bed, has a band of gold leaf with an inner cartouche formed by two branches, showing a song thrush against a gold background. The dark blue band provides a strong contrast to the light blue field within the panel.

. . .

RIGHT: Sketch of bed with headboard in place.

LEFT: This headboard for a child's bed depicts the dawn chorus. The choir consists, from left to right, of a sparrow, a curl bunting, a yellow wagtail, a meadow pipit and a willow warbler. The conductor is a blackbird. Branches frame both panel and landscape, with the sun rising in the background.

○   ○   ○

RIGHT: Study of a nightingale. This bird would be a good subject for a headboard, possibly for an insomniac, as he or she could then imagine the drowsy atmosphere of a garden on a warm summer's evening, filled with the song of the nightingale.

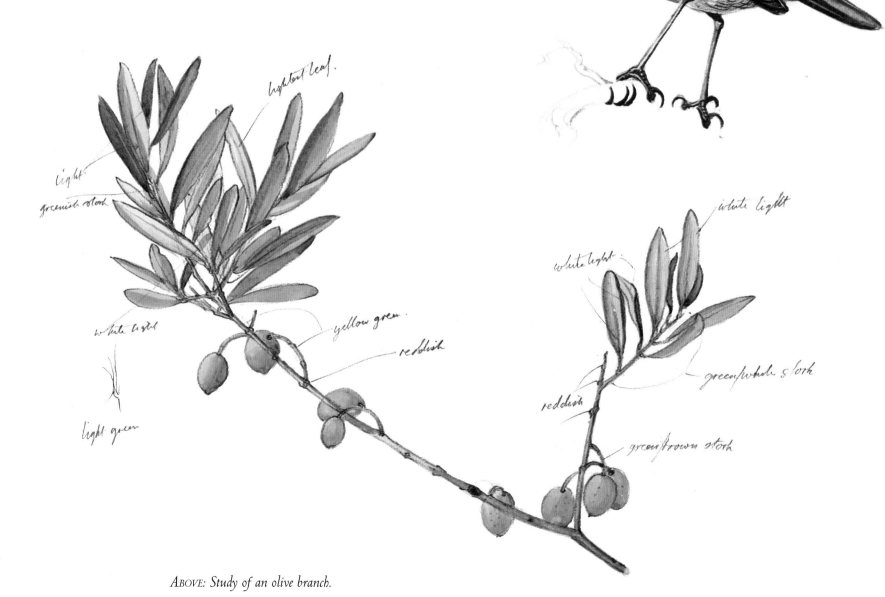

ABOVE: Study of an olive branch.

Classical subjects such as the one depicted on the headboard above can be very effective. Here, Pan is chasing the nymph Syrinx. In the legend, Syrinx prayed to be transformed to avoid capture and Pan found himself clutching an armful of reeds. When the wind blew through the reeds, the sound pleased Pan so much that he cut some reeds and made himself a set of pipes, which are named after the nymph. They are shown here in a *trompe l'oeil* effect, as though Pan is himself in the bed and has hung up his pipes for safekeeping.

◦　◦　◦

ABOVE: This headboard is designed for a double bed. It is painted in grisaille on a board cut in an auricular shape.

RIGHT: The design for this headboard is based on a marble relief depicting Night by the Danish neo-classical sculptor Bertel Alberto Thovaldson.

*ABOVE: This design can be adapted to the letter or monogram of your choice. For a child's
headboard, for example, the initial letter of the first name could be decorated with an image
appropriate to the name's meaning such as a bee for Melissa, a horse's head for Philippa or a
crown for Stephen.*

o   o   o

*LEFT: This night-blooming cereus, also known as the moon cactus, is taken from Philip Reinagle's
painting of the same subject in Thornton's* Temple of Flora.

ABOVE: This monogram was inspired by the nineteenth-century decorative 'animal' alphabet shown opposite. The name of the bed's occupant can be written on the ribbon below the cartouche.

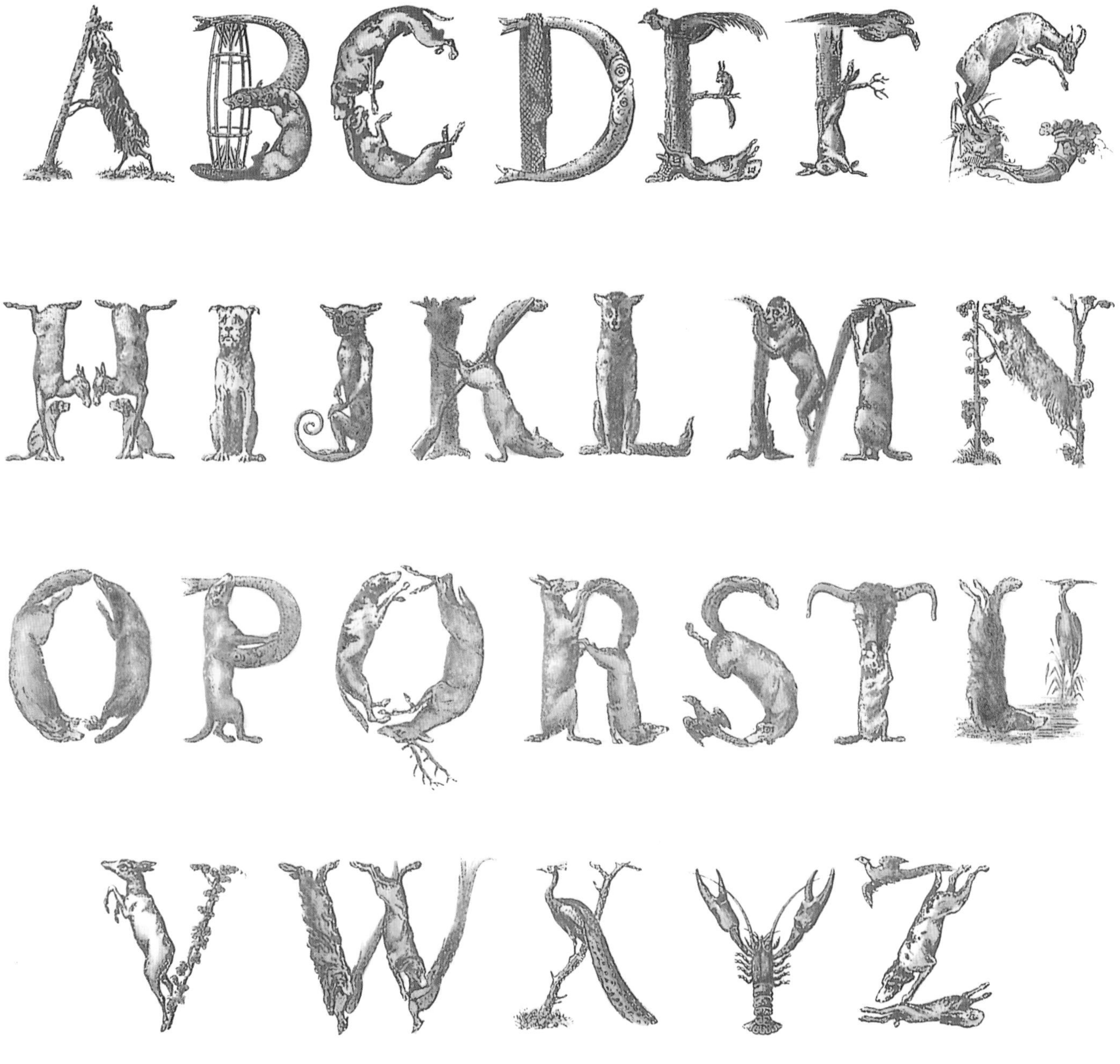
ABCDEFG
HIJKLMN
OPQRSTU
VWXYZ

Dog Kennels and Beds

· · · · ·

I first had the idea for these decorated dog kennels after seeing a beautifully painted eighteenth-century dog's bed. Ornamental kennels and beds for both dogs and cats were popular amongst the French aristocracy at that time — both the Marquise de Pompadour and Queen Marie Antoinette are known to have commissioned them for their favourite pets. Clearly, they are not appropriate for outdoor use, and their design makes them more suitable for Pugs or toy dogs than for larger breeds such as Labradors or Great Danes.

· · ·

Left: One of the magenta panels for the kennel shown opposite.

Right: A scallop-tiled, domed kennel in grey with gilded decoration.

ABOVE: This kennel is an attempt to combine decoration, in the form of a miniature neo-Gothic folly, with additional practicality, in the form of an upholstered seat.

BELOW: This simple bed is for the dog who does not like to sleep in an enclosed space. An alternative to the handle would be the dog's name painted on the back panel in an oval as shown above.

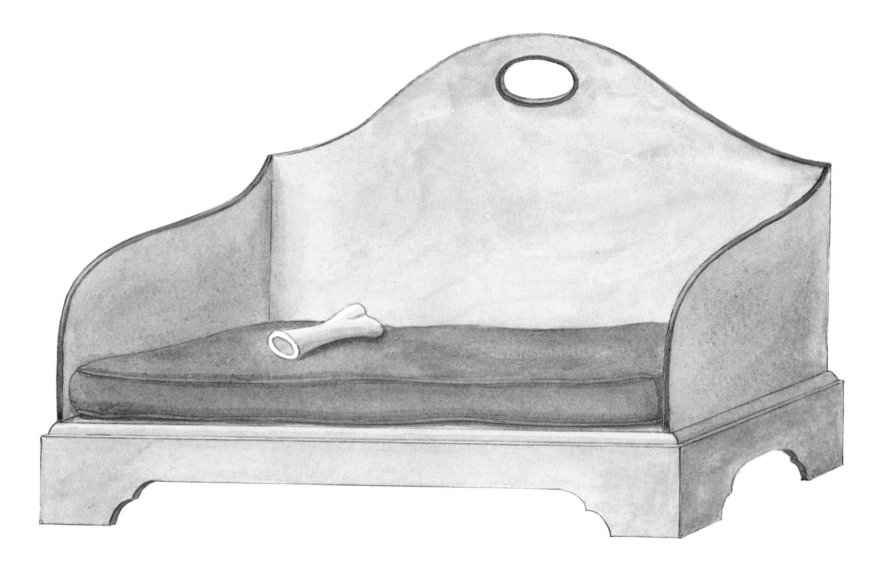

Left: This kennel was inspired by the Chinese pavilion at Sans Souci which I painted when in Berlin. It would be a ideal home for an Oriental breed of small dog such as a Pekingese, a Shih Tzu or a Lhasa Apso.

o o o

Below: This bed is also in the Chinese style, although much simpler. The only decoration is the suggestion of panels in trompe l'oeil.

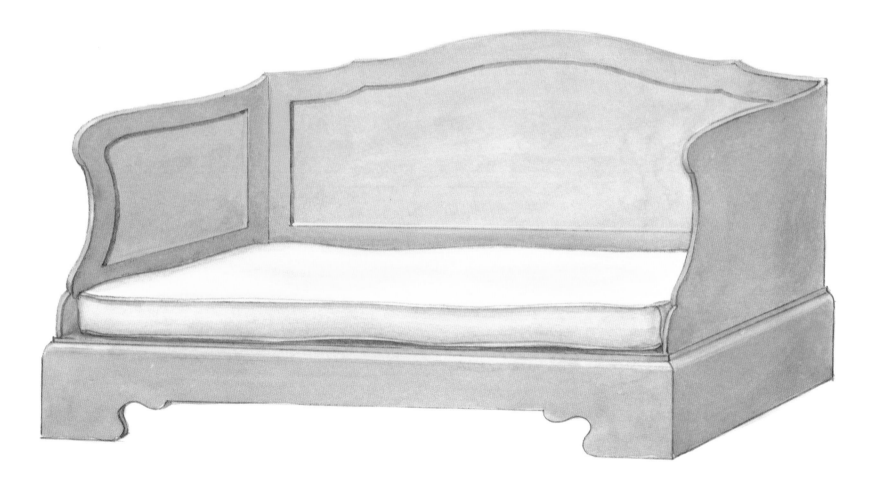

TWO TABLES

. . . .

54

The coffee table shown here was commissioned by Lord and Lady Hertford for the library at their home, Ragley Hall in Warwickshire *(see page 137)*. They particularly wanted it to echo the design of the eighteenth-century chimneypiece, which is made of green and white Connemara marble. The surface of this table, which, like the commode on page 34, was made by Maurice Hurst in his Suffolk workshop, is a slab of the same marble and the frame has been painted by Ros Hornak in *trompe l'oeil* marble to match.

. . .

BELOW: Sketches showing the unpainted and finished table frames.

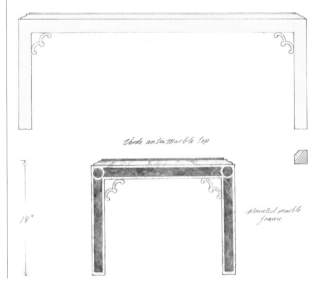

RIGHT: A design for an astrological table. The outer circle is made up of the twelve signs of the Zodiac. The central image here is Aquarius, the water carrier, but it could be replaced by any sign you wish. Surrounding Aquarius is the night sky, showing the exact disposition of the stars at the time of the owner's birth.

24" dia.

56

When I was painting in Jaipur in 1975 I bought a marvellous ivory chess set. When the pieces proved to be larger than the board I had at home, I decided to make my own board. Finally, twenty years later, this plan has been realized. The new board is made out of semi-precious stones to a design which I created in collaboration with Rui Paes. We wanted to make something that would echo the mogul design of the ivory figures, something with that richness and brightness which is quintessentially Indian. We kept to a simple geometric design in order to show off the stones themselves: bloodstone, malachite, tiger iron, turquoise, jade, chrysokoll, tiger's eye and lapis lazuli. The border is made of black agate and red jasper, the squares are of red jasper and chalcedony, and the water-gilded frame is supported by four winged ormolu feet. The gilded support is ideal for placing the board on a table, but the design could just as well be set into a specially designed surface. The board was made in Idar Oberstein in Germany, which is renowned for the expertise of its stone cutters. The craftsmen took enormous care — and many hours — to produce an immaculate finish.

Although this chessboard is made of inlaid semi-precious stones, a similar effect could be obtained by a skilful use of *trompe l'oeil*. A painted panel of wood with a coating of gesso would facilitate a highly polished finish for a fraction of the cost of the stones.

BELOW: The working sketch for the chessboard. The board is mounted on a granite base and has a gilded frame.

ABOVE: The finished chessboard displaying some of the set for which it was created. The chess pieces have an Indian interpretation: the king and queen are riding in howdahs on elephants and the bishop is a camel!

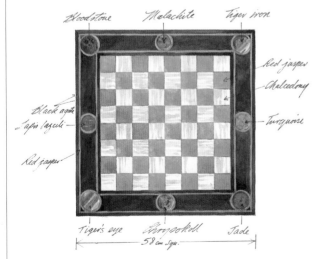

Right: The frame of the board is supported at each corner by a winged ormolu foot.

TABLEWARE

This chapter contains designs for plates, placemats and trays. The designs for china can be used to make matching sets of identical plates, or a single decorative element, such as a border, may be extracted and used with a series of central images. These could follow a culinary theme, such as mushrooms, nuts or summer fruits.

PLACEMATS

· · · · ·

The placemats in this chapter are of three basic shapes: circular, octagonal and rectangular. All of the designs shown here could easily be adapted to fit any one of these shapes, as could the designs for plates and trays.

· · ·

RIGHT: A study of a Regal Thorny oyster. These particular oysters, which are found in the Philippines, have delightfully contrasting inner and outer textures. They are not, however, edible.

LEFT: This design for a rectangular placemat uses the oyster as a centrepiece, surrounded by a border of seaweed and pearls.

· · ·

RIGHT: Studies of seaweed. This leaf-like variety is very useful as "foliage" for any border or cartouche with a marine theme.

ABOVE: *This design shows the young Bacchus crowned with vine leaves, enjoying the fruits of the harvest amidst the vineyards at the Quinta de Vargelas, attended by* putti *and a dancing fawn.*

The two placemats shown here (*LEFT AND RIGHT*) were commissioned by Taylor's Port as part of the celebration for the company's tercentenary in 1992. Taylor's name and motif is shown in a cartouche above each landscape. If you want to add something personal to a design, this is a neat and effective way to incorporate a monogram, crest or motto.

A border of gilded vine leaves and grapes on a purple background encircles two vistas of the river Douro in Portugal, one in Oporto and the other further up the Douro valley at Vargelas. The god Bacchus represents the young wine, and his elderly lieutenant Silenus personifies the mature vintage.

The surface of the mats has been laminated so that it can withstand heat and stains and be wiped clean.

. . .

RIGHT: *At Taylor's lodge on the bank of the Douro, the garlanded Silenus, helped by* putti *and a pipe-playing fawn, is tasting the wine. Mid-ground, a "rabelo" boat carries the casks to the lodge, and in the distance is the Dom Luis bridge, which links Gaia and Oporto.*

To make a placemat, it is not necessary to paint straight onto hardboard. It is far simpler to reproduce your original line drawing on paper, paint it, and then laminate it onto the board. Lamination is, in any case, essential, to prevent the mat from being stained. The edge of the placemat can then be gilded, and the back covered in felt. The placemat is then ready for use.

o   o   o

BELOW: Study of a lemon. A partly peeled lemon gives an interesting contrast of three very different textures: skin, pith and flesh. If you have chosen a piece of fruit or a vegetable as the central image for your placemat or plate, it should not be reproduced larger than life size, as this may look rather grotesque. Like several of the studies of fruit, vegetables and shellfish shown in this chapter, this lemon was originally painted as part of a series of illustrations which I contributed to The Fine Art of Dining, *a collection of recipes by world-famous chefs. The book is sold to benefit the Elizabeth FitzRoy Homes, which care for those with profound learning disabilities.*

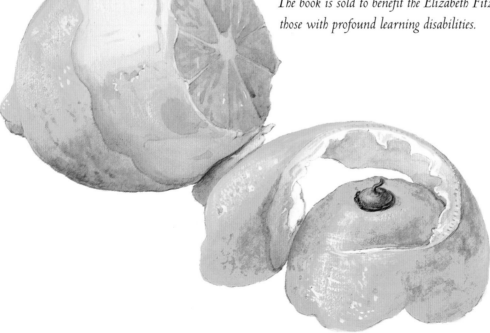

ABOVE: The half-peeled lemons are shown on a black background with a Venetian red border decorated with strips of peel. Black and red provide a strong contrast to the citrus yellow of the fruit's skin.

Above: Here, I have painted the orange segments on a placemat with black lacquer background and a trompe l'oeil inlay of green jade. This treatment would be equally suitable for the lemons shown on page 63.

BELOW: Study of an orange. An amusing idea for a set of placemats is a citrus theme, with oranges and lemons alternating round the dinner table. Other attractive themes might be summer fruits or exotic fruits such as mango, papaya and star-fruit. Leaves of the represented fruits could decorate the border of each placemat.

ABOVE: The ingredients of a Chinese salad, with a red pepper at the centre, form the decoration in this design for a circular mat.

CERAMIC PLATES

· · · · ·

I first became involved in designs for ceramic plates through the Queen Elizabeth Foundation for the Disabled. The idea was to design a collection of plates depicting famous country houses in England and Scotland which could then be made in the Foundation's own workshops and sold in the gift shops of those of the houses open to the public.

The first set of ten designs was executed in black and white on octagonal plates with the crest of the house's owner on the rim. I produced a design in black and white which was then made into a transfer and fired onto a ready-glazed plate. Sepia designs were also drawn in black and white and then printed in colour. Some of the designs in this chapter could be reproduced in this way, but others require more sophisticated methods, and one or two would need to be painted by hand for the best effect.

LEFT AND ABOVE: The houses shown here are the English Arundel Castle, West Sussex; Chatsworth House, Derbyshire (on the opposite page), and (clockwise from top left), Hatfield House, Hertfordshire; Harewood House, West Yorkshire; Bowood House, Wiltshire and lastly Inveraray Castle, which is in Scotland.

68

ABOVE: Other plates I have designed include this single one depicting Chequers, the Prime Minister's official country house in Buckinghamshire, England, in ink and wash. This was commissioned by the then Prime Minister Margaret Thatcher, both for use and to give as souvenirs to visiting dignitaries.

. . .

After the set of octagonal plates, I also designed a set of six circular plates (BELOW AND RIGHT) for the Queen Elizabeth Foundation for the Disabled. These have sanguine-coloured vignettes of noted English and Scottish country houses with the owner's crest in gold, and a gold rim around the edge of the plate.

. . .

Shown below is Sudeley Castle, Gloucestershire, opposite are (clockwise from top left); The Great Conservatory, Syon Park, London; Blenheim Palace, Oxfordshire; Hever Castle, Kent; Clandon Park, Surrey; and Balmoral Castle, Grampian, Scotland.

ABOVE: *Château Cos d'Estournel a second-growth château.*

After the country house plates, I produced another set, depicting six wine-producing châteaux in the Médoc area of the Bordeaux region of France. They were executed in a monochrome of umber in rococo cartouches on round plates. I intend to follow these with plates showing châteaux in other wine-growing areas of France, perhaps for a set of dessert plates featuring châteaux which specialize in dessert wines.

BELOW: *The figure of Bacchus, printed in gold, was an appropriate unifying motif for this set of plates.*

Above: Château Mouton-Rothschild, Château Latour, Château Margaux and Château Lafite-Rothschild are all first-growth châteaux, Château Cos d'Estournel is second growth and Château Beychevelle, fourth growth.

ABOVE: This is one of a limited edition of 50 plates showing the birthplace of the painter Thomas Gainsborough in Sudbury, Suffolk. It was made to coincide with an exhibition I had at Gainsborough's House Museum. The palette symbolizes the artist's profession.

In 1981, I visited the Holy Land, inspired by the journey of the artist David Roberts. I aimed to re-trace his steps and paint many of the same views that he painted in 1839. I had varying degrees of success in this: the political situation in Egypt and the Lebanon ruled out some of the sites, and others no longer existed, having been buried under concrete and tarmac. However, much help and hospitality was given in Jordan, where the government of HM King Hussein generously arranged for me to stay at Petra and Akaba. As a gesture of thanks, I designed a plate for His Majesty, using my painting of the escutcheon on the fort at Akaba as the central image.

BELOW: One of the designs I made for the Akaba plate.

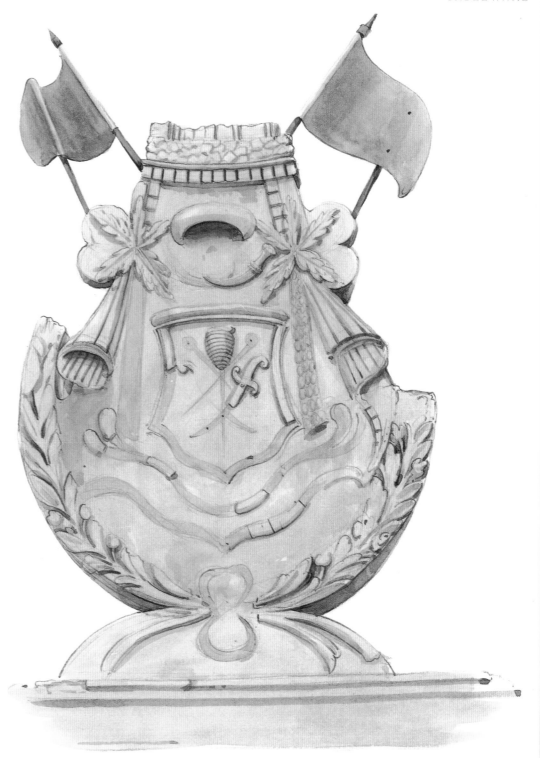

ABOVE: Roberts' grandiose view of the fort at Akaba had filled me with expectation — in reality, the crumbling remains of the building were so obscured by palm trees that I drove past them several times without realizing what they were! I spent a precarious afternoon on the top of a ricketty ladder, painting this escutcheon, which is above the fort's main gate.

LEFT: I painted this study of mushrooms for one of a series of six plates with the theme of edible fungi. These field mushrooms, and others like the silky beige oyster mushrooms with their grey frills, or knobby black Italian summer truffles, will be much more rewarding to paint than the ubiquitous white button mushrooms.

. . .

RIGHT: The bumpy cauliflower with its rugged texture is also a good monochromatic subject and provides a good contrast to the smooth skin of the mushroom. The leaves of the cauliflower feature in the window panel design on page 161.

. . .

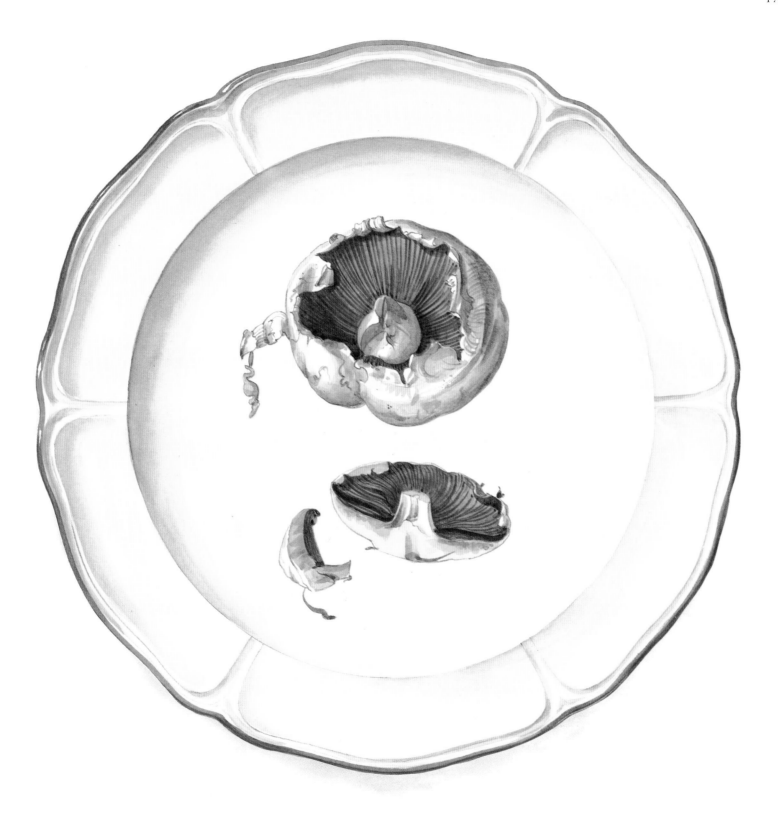

*ABOVE: This plate is an eighteenth-century Wedgwood design, measuring nine inches in diameter. I have
added a plain chestnut-coloured band around the rim.*

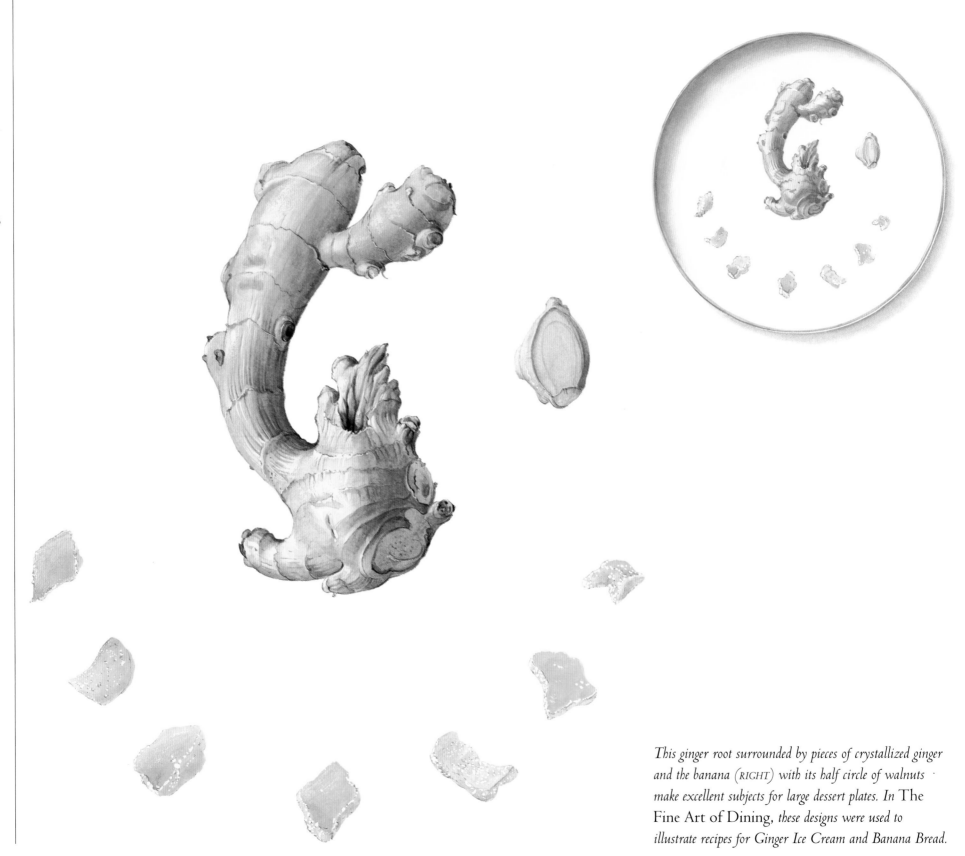

This ginger root surrounded by pieces of crystallized ginger and the banana (RIGHT) with its half circle of walnuts make excellent subjects for large dessert plates. In The Fine Art of Dining, *these designs were used to illustrate recipes for Ginger Ice Cream and Banana Bread.*

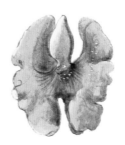

The citrus fruit designs used in the placemats on pages 62 and 65 could also be used for dessert plates, as could berries and orchard fruits.

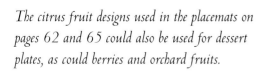

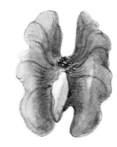

TRAYS

. . . . .

Like placemats, trays are usually one of three basic shapes – circular, oval or rectangular – and the designs shown on the following pages may be adapted accordingly. This design of snails and garlic was adapted to decorate the plain rectangular wooden tray shown opposite, but it would work equally successfully with a round or oval one. Any tray runs the risk of damage from hot dishes or spilt liquids, so the surface should always be laminated for protection before it is put to use.

. . .

Left: In this design, flat-leaf parsley is surrounded by snails and snail shells, garlic bulbs and a shallot.

*ABOVE: I have modified my original design (*LEFT*) to accommodate this rectangular tray.*

LEFT: The lobster still life is reproduced in an oval panel in the centre of a tin tray. As it is a relatively complicated composition with many different elements, I have chosen a simple background, painting the tray cream and adding a trellis pattern, resembling a fishing net, in blue.

o o o

BELOW: Study of a lobster. The colour and anatomical structure of these crustaceans make them particularly appealing to draw and paint.

LEFT: My intention here was to try to include elements which were both decorative and edible, such as the yellow marrow flower, the curling lemon peel and the bulb of fennel, grouping them around the central image of the lobster and thus turning the composition into a colourful still life.

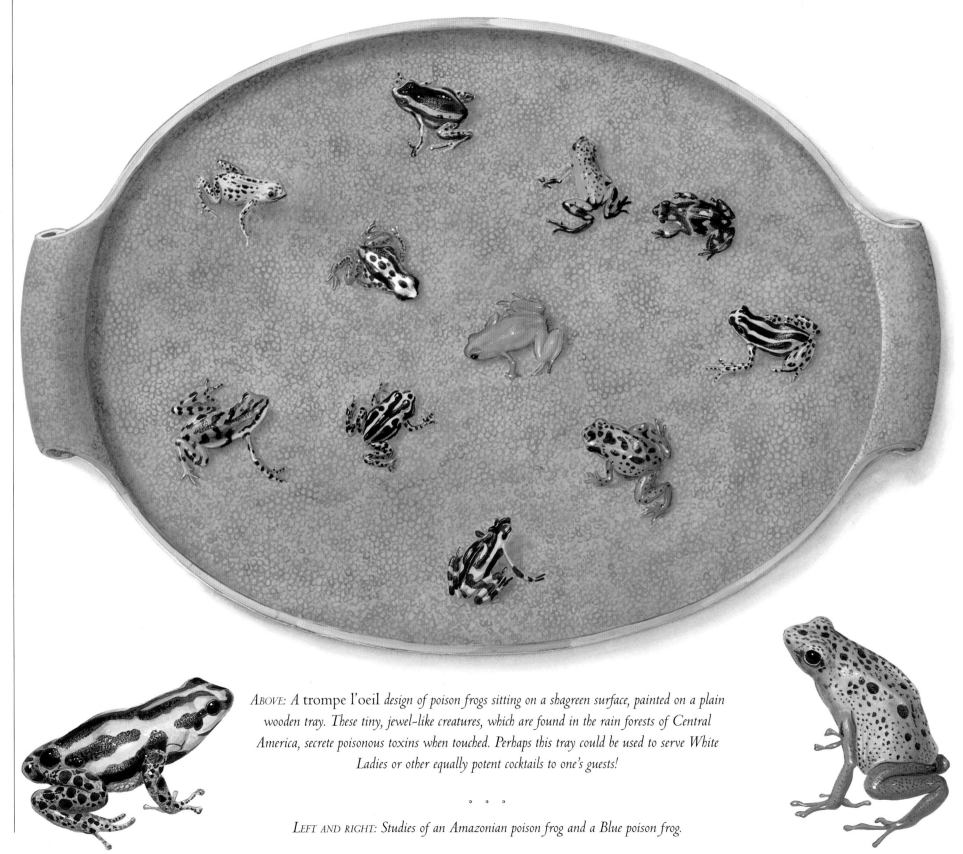

ABOVE: A trompe l'oeil *design of poison frogs sitting on a shagreen surface, painted on a plain wooden tray. These tiny, jewel-like creatures, which are found in the rain forests of Central America, secrete poisonous toxins when touched. Perhaps this tray could be used to serve White Ladies or other equally potent cocktails to one's guests!*

• • •

LEFT AND RIGHT: Studies of an Amazonian poison frog and a Blue poison frog.

ABOVE: This wooden tray is also painted in trompe l'oeil *to look as though the monogram in ivory is let into a shagreen surface.*

ABOVE: The design of this black lacquer papier mâché *tray is taken from a Portuguese eighteenth-century* Companhia das Indias *plate. I added the discarded artichoke leaves to the border.*

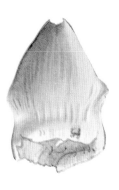

BELOW: The little basket containing the artichokes is a miniature example of a Portuguese canastra. *Fishermen's wives have traditionally used these to carry the catch to market, balancing the flat, fish-filled baskets on their heads, and then used them to arrange picturesque displays to tempt the customers.*

RIGHT: I made various studies of artichokes and artichoke leaves before deciding on an image. Like cabbages, artichokes are wonderfully enticing sculptural objects, and easy to obtain.

ABOVE: I made this study of Highgrove in Gloucestershire for a painting that was commissioned as a present for its owner, HRH the Prince of Wales. I have painted the background of the tray, shown left, as a trompe l'oeil *marquetry veneer of inlaid wood.*

CUSHIONS
AND OTHER SMALL OBJECTS

THIS CHAPTER INCLUDES DESIGNS FOR JEWELLERY AS WELL AS SMALLER DECORATED PIECES SUCH AS BOXES, CLOCKS AND PAPERWEIGHTS. THE CUSHION DESIGNS ARE INTENDED TO BE PAINTED ON SILK, BUT THEY COULD BE RENDERED IN NEEDLEPOINT ON CANVAS EQUALLY EFFECTIVELY. WHERE POSSIBLE, LINE DRAWINGS OF THE DESIGNS ARE INCLUDED FOR TRACING.

88

ENAMEL PLAQUES

. . . . .

I was commissioned by The Halcyon Days Enamel Company to produce designs for a limited edition of two framed plaques shown here. The designs were initially transfer-printed in outline onto the enamelled copper panels and then painstakingly painted before being fired. Enamelling has been popular in England since the eighteenth century and it is an art in itself, requiring a high degree of skill and technical knowledge, since the colours used change dramatically during the firing process, which is done at around 800 degrees centigrade.

. . .

LEFT: Wearing a jewelled collar, this cheetah sits in a classical landscape, surrounded by a baroque cartouche.

RIGHT: The companion piece is a leopard in a similar landscape with an identical cartouche. The two plaques could either sit on small easels on a table or hang on the wall.

ENAMEL BOXES

These small enamel boxes were also commissioned by Halcyon Days. Boxes like these, decorated with pictures or messages, have been popular for over two hundred years, and the earliest examples are now much valued by collectors. For such a small surface area, the designs have to be chosen with care and the subjects should be as small and delicate as the boxes they adorn. Flowers, small birds and insects would all work well in this format, and should you wish to create a series of boxes, butterflies and moths can be particularly attractive to paint.

The bee and strawberry shown here make a happy, summer motif, and the frog with his golden ball was inspired by the well-known fairy story The Frog Prince.

ABOVE: Colour studies and line drawings for an oval box. This cyclamen is a good example of an intricate plant which nevertheless works well in the small space available. The designs shown here are reproduced at twice their original size.

LEFT AND RIGHT: Colour study and line drawing of an auricula. This was adapted from a watercolour (not shown) for an oval box design. The flowerpot had to be considerably reduced in size to prevent it from being too dominant.

o   o   o

Long before I painted the picture opposite, the image of a baby cradled in a rose was one that I wished to develop. I used the same image, this time without the halo, for the enamel boxes shown here, as I thought it would make a charming gift for the mother of a new-born child. Halcyon Days decided to make two different reproductions of the image: one with a pink rose, for a girl, and one with a blue rose, for a boy.

o   o   o

*ABOVE: My original picture of the infant Jesus lying in a rose. I painted the background of the night sky
with a waning moon in order to suggest the dawning of a new era heralded by the birth of Christ.*

CLOCK

○ ○ ○ ○ ○

RIGHT: These two young toads with a dandelion would be an appropriate subject for a clock in a child's bedroom, especially if he or she is learning to tell the time. The individual seeds of the dandelion, blown into the air, mark the position of the numbers on the clock's face.

○ ○ ○

LEFT: I designed the painting specially to fit this octagonal wooden clock case, which has been stippled in umber and then partially gilded.

JEWELLERY

∘ ∘ ∘ ∘ ∘

While working in Germany at Büdingen, I visited Idar Oberstein, the world centre for precious stones. Inspired by pieces in the museum, Rui Paes and I worked on this design for a tiara. The long and difficult task of making it has been undertaken in Sweden by Rui's sister Andrea Paes.

∘ ∘ ∘

BELOW: The watercolour of the design for the tiara. The design is based on a Peacock butterfly, recreated in aquamarines, diamonds and pearls, with four pear-shaped South Sea pearls. The front of the tiara is executed in white gold and the reverse in yellow gold. In order to maximize the use of this piece — for tiaras are not worn very often — the central butterfly is detachable and may be used as a brooch. The two larger South Sea pearl drops and river diamonds are also detachable and may be used as earrings.

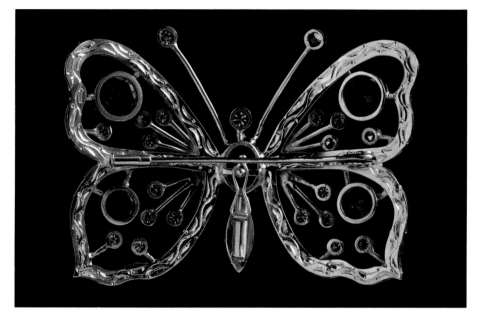

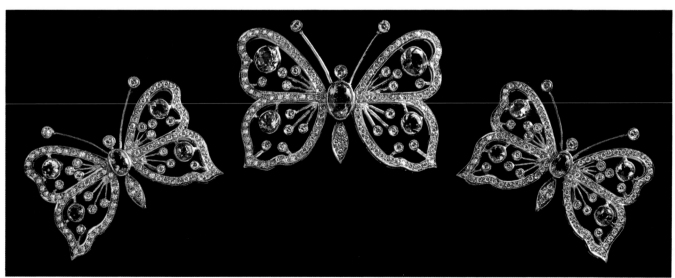

ABOVE: Work is in progress on the tiara — so far, the three butterflies have been completed.

PAPERWEIGHTS

· · · · ·

Whilst working in Germany I came across Eberhard Bank, one of the world's foremost carvers of precious stones. I commissioned him to carve a snail to my design, with the intention of using it as part of a paperweight. Herr Bank made this wonderful snail (BELOW) out of a single piece of lapis lazuli, somehow contriving to fashion the animal's shell out of the blue and gold portion of the stone, and its head and body out of the paler part.

· · ·

RIGHT: My idea for a paperweight is to position the snail so that it appears to be making its way over rocky ground, leaving its silvery trail — made out of diamonds — in its wake. The base of the paperweight will be modelled in wax and then cast in gold. To give it weight, the inside of the base will be filled with heavy sand in a chamois-leather bag

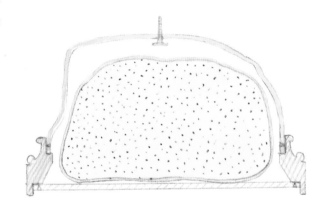

BELOW: Two views of the lapis lazuli snail.

ABOVE AND RIGHT: A rhinoceros, made by Hermann Petrie in labradorite, forms the centrepiece of this paperweight. The creature is standing on a base of gold, set with "pebbles" made of pink cabouchon sapphires.

· · ·

BELOW: Another idea for an animal paperweight. Despite the injunction "cast not your pearls before swine," pigs and pearls are a good match. I plan to have the pig carved in rose quartz, with four pearls on a gold base.

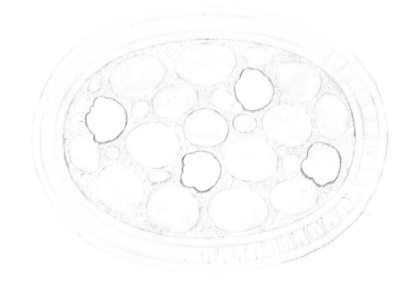

CUSHIONS

· · · · ·

The centrepiece of this cushion design (LEFT) shows my French bulldog Bella sitting in a rococo cartouche surrounded by sea shells, pearls and a bee, all on a background of yellow with a trellis pattern. The design was originally intended to be painted on silk in the manner of the cyclamen shown on page 103, but here it has been interpreted for needlepoint by Kathleen Mackenzie and expertly sewn by Cathy Gaynor using 86 different-coloured wools and cottons (RIGHT). The design is shown in outline overleaf.

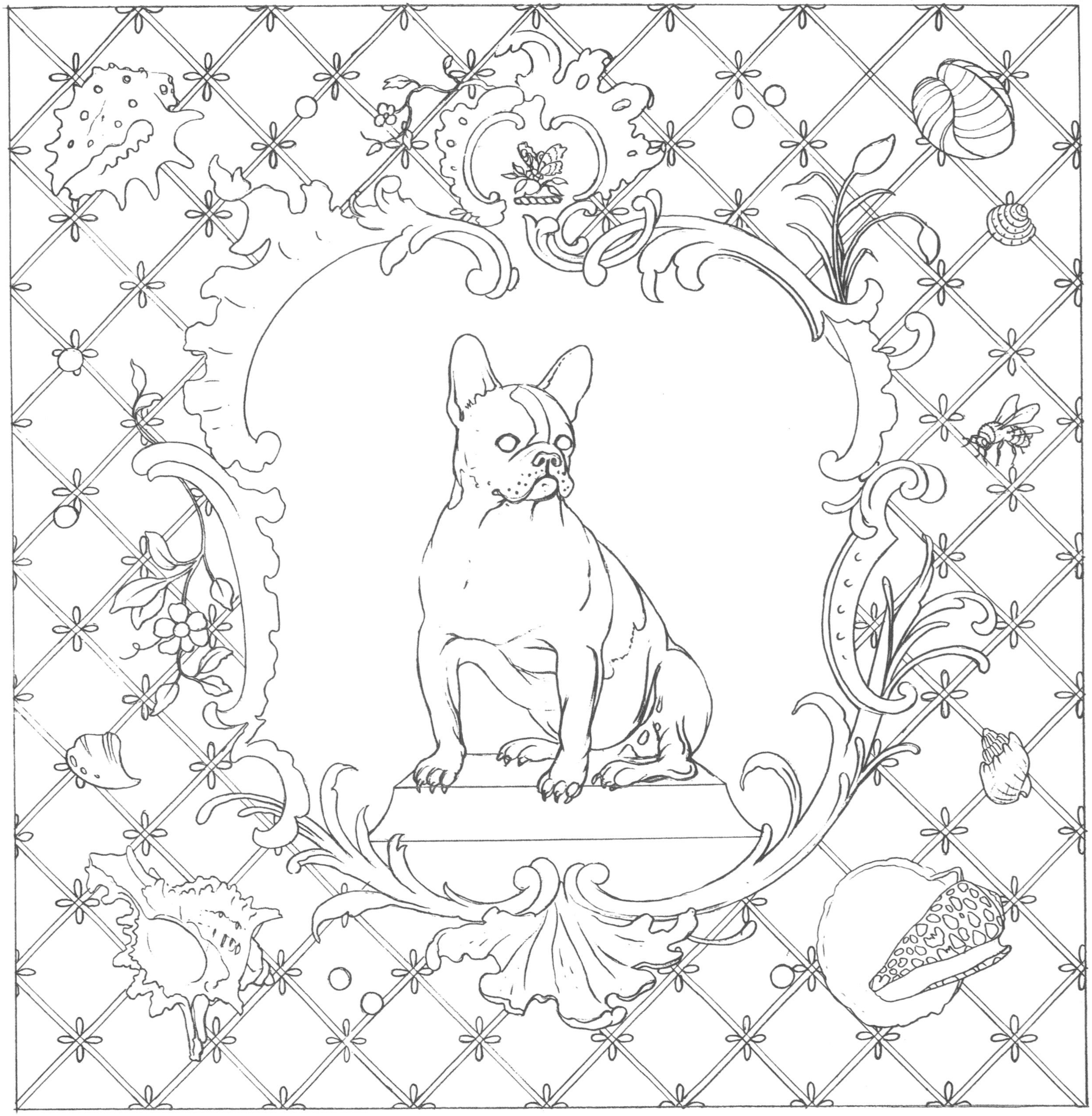

ABOVE: This design of a cyclamen (SEE OVER) in a Gothick panel was executed by Rui Paes on a cream silk cushion.

ABOVE AND RIGHT: Studies for a pair of cyclamen. These two paintings were originally done to be reproduced as a limited edition for the Racing and Breeding Fine Arts Fund, but I decided that they would also make an attractive pair of cushion covers.

RIGHT AND OPPOSITE: If you wish to paint a cushion with a flower design, you might find this sunflower a good place to start. The image is strong and graphic and lends itself to being simplified or stylized more easily than complex flower forms such as the cyclamen on the previous page.

Below: I suppose that this barnacle, which I painted in the South of France, might seem an unusual choice for a cushion, but a series of cushions with a marine theme, such as the one shown opposite, would be delightful, especially for a house or cottage by the sea. Over the years I have amassed a large collection of shells and pieces of coral as I find them a great source of inspiration.

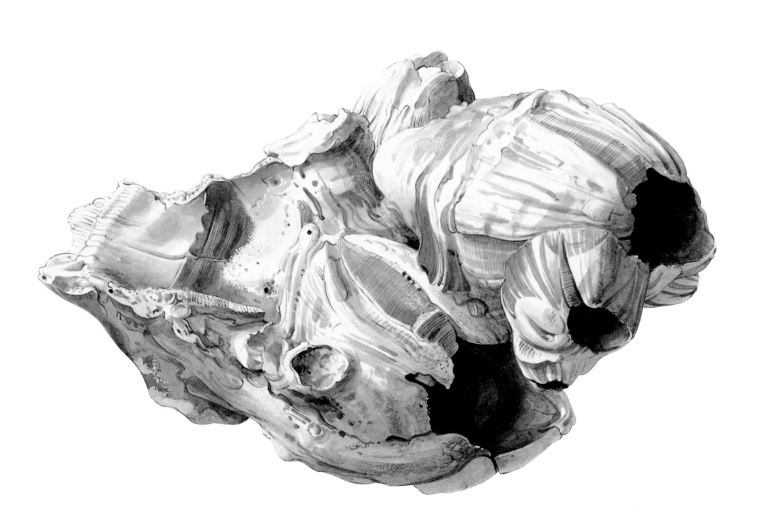

III

Although orange is not everyone's favourite colour, using a single graphic image like this pumpkin or crab is an excellent way to give punch in certain decorative schemes.

. . .

LEFT: This distinctively shaped "pumpkin" is actually a decorative gourd called a Turk's cap. I bought it in a market at Cogolin in the south of France, attracted by its texture and bright colour.

. . .

RIGHT: Study for a crab cushion. The crab is holding a pearl between its claws, and a number of smaller pearls appear on the sandy background.

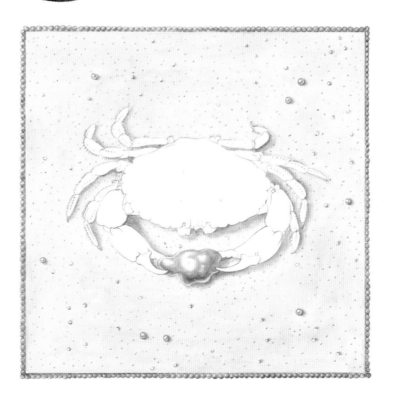

LEFT: The delightful potager *of the Château de Villandry in the Loire Valley is a wonderful source of inspiration to anyone who enjoys drawing and painting vegetables. In my design, the garden is surrounded by a cartouche of the different vegetables that are grown in it, as well as a couple of pests — the cabbage white butterfly and the Colorado beetle.*

. . .

ABOVE AND LEFT: Based on the well-known fairytale, this cushion would be a good present for any Cinderella! This intricate design, however, would be extremely difficult to reproduce by any other method than painting and is not an ideal subject for a cushion unless you are adept at working on silk and have great patience.

. . .

RIGHT: I completed studies of many different flowers before deciding which blooms to include in the cartouche.

Nyman's garden, created in 1890 by Ludwig Messel and subsequently restored by the Earl and Countess of Rosse, is one of the great gardens of the Sussex Weald, with rare plants from all over the world. The design on the opposite page shows a monochromatic view of the romantic ruins of Nyman's, which was destroyed by fire, surrounded by a cartouche of the different types of flowers grown in the beautiful herbaceous borders.

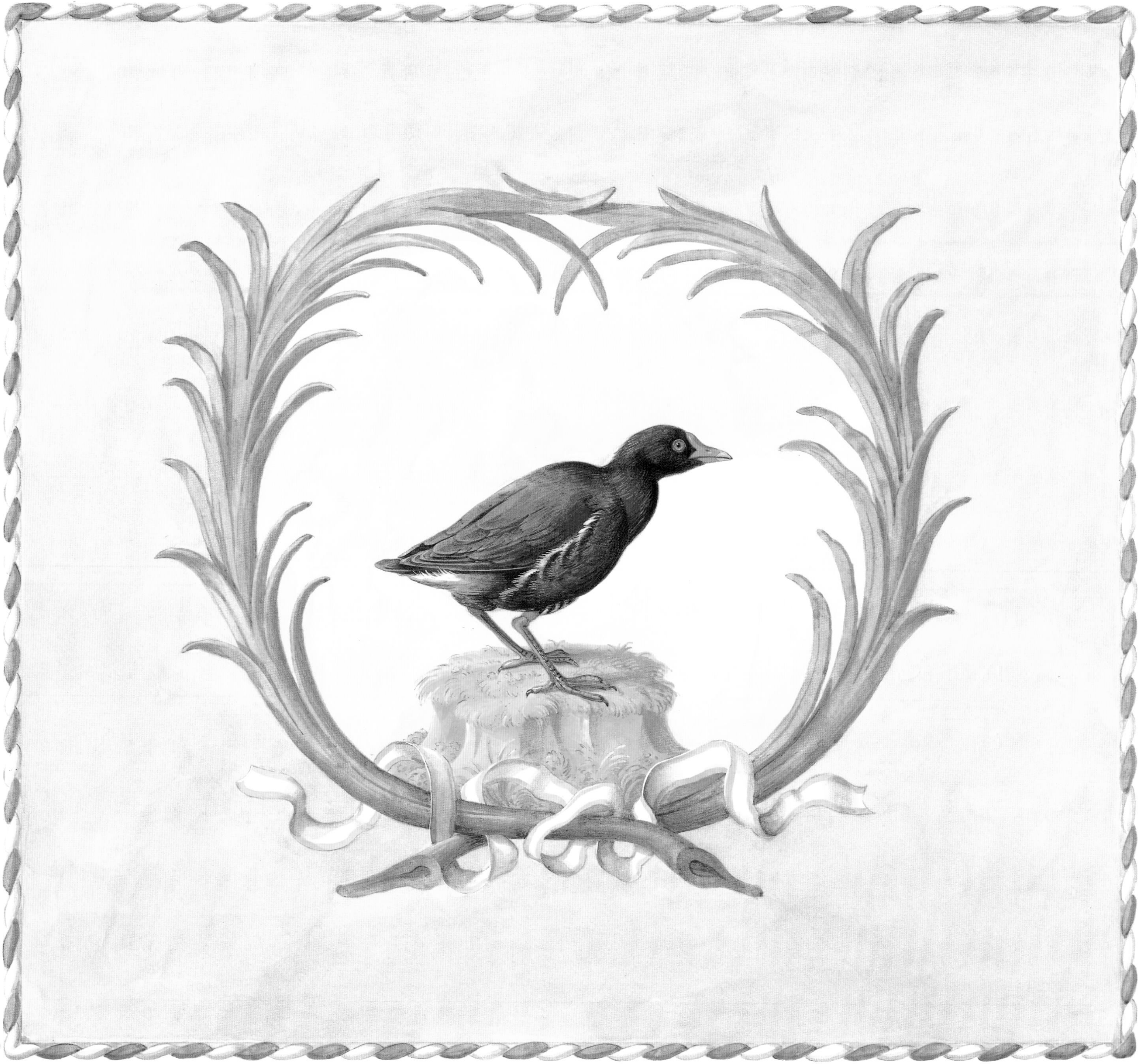

LEFT: *I have several moorhens living on the pond in my garden and with them in mind I created this design for a cushion showing one in a cartouche of reeds. This treatment would be an appropriate one for any waterfowl. For birds who live on the land, a central image showing the subject on a nest with a cartouche of branches and twigs might work well.*

ABOVE: *Letter designs can be as simple or as intricate as you like, and can be rendered in a variety of media. Here, the initial "A" is painted on white linen in a manner that suggests embroidery. The needle, also painted in* trompe l'oeil *with a piece of thread hanging from it, suggests that the embroiderer has just finished sewing.*

ABOVE AND RIGHT: The horticultural trophy in the centre of this design shows a beetroot and a dibber with a length of twine wrapped around it. The border, composed of oyster shells, scallop shells and seaweed, is reminiscent of a seaside garden, where shells and other treasures of the sea are used as decorative edging for flower beds and paths.

Auriculas reached the height of their popularity in Europe at the end of the eighteenth century, when auricula shows were held and the rich proudly displayed their auricula "theatres" – massed plants on tiers of velvet-draped shelves, with mirrors placed behind them to reflect their beauty. The popularity of auriculas diminished in the nineteenth century, but they have recently come back into fashion, and hybrids are being produced in ever greater numbers.

Left: For those who wish to take time over their painting, the auricula is an ideal subject because as long as the plant is well cared-for, its succulent leaves will not wilt or change their shape.

Right: This auricula, shown in a panel, could be painted on silk or executed in needlepoint.

CARDS AND LABELS

THIS CHAPTER INCLUDES DESIGNS WHICH CAN BE ADAPTED FOR A RANGE OF ITEMS FROM WRITING PAPER, POSTCARDS AND BOOKPLATES TO MENU COVERS, WINE LABELS AND GAME CARDS. MANY OF THESE DESIGNS ARE OF A PERSONAL NATURE, AND PART OF THE CHALLENGE IN PAINTING THEM LIES IN CREATING A VISUAL UNITY FROM THE DIVERSE ASPECTS OF THE RECIPIENT'S CHARACTER AND INTERESTS.

CARTOUCHES

○ ○ ○ ○ ○

A house can be an important personal symbol, especially if it has been owned by the same family for many generations and has become the repository of its history. For this reason, I am often asked to make people's homes the focus of items such as bookplates and letter-heads. It is sometimes difficult to produce a single, definitive image of a house. Some houses, like some people, have "best sides" and lend themselves very much to a single view. Others, however, have front and rear façades so different in character that it is hard to believe that they are part of the same building. In these cases, one must either produce two views or try to represent, perhaps with other elements, the full character of the property. Whether I paint the houses in colour or not depends on the feeling I want to convey in the picture. If they are not painted in colour, I generally choose a monochrome of black, so that they can then be reproduced in any other single colour. An example of this is the postcard of the Château de Thoiry on page 136, where the original has been reproduced in four different colours.

Architectural designs and plasterwork have provided me with reference material for many of the decorative devices in this chapter. I have also drawn inspiration from the pattern books and furniture designs of Chippendale, Heppelwhite and Kent, among others. I often photograph or sketch architectural details on my travels, which are then filed away for use at a later date.

I have used this drawing of the Old Rectory, Somerton, Suffolk, as both a postcard and a letterhead. A different view of the same house is incorporated into my bookplate on page 140.

This is a good example of how a single design can be used in two entirely different ways. I was asked by Mrs Martyn Hedley to paint the family's cottage as a birthday present for her husband. In earlier times a coastguard's cottage, it sits on the promontory of Constantine Bay in Cornwall facing the sea.

I decided to paint the cottage and landscape in monochrome and introduce colour for the cartouche only. The cartouche has a marine theme, with illustrations of shells and seaweed that I collected from the beach. The mythology of the sea is represented by mermaids, with a string of pearls depicting its treasures. I included the shrimping nets to evoke happy memories of childhood holidays by the sea.

. . .

LEFT: This Constantine Bay label is intended as a pun — the wine inside the bottle comes not from Cornwall, but from a French vineyard called Château Constantine.

ABOVE: Studies of Cornish seaweed.

The original painting measures 14″ x 18″ and has been reduced for use both as a post-card and as a wine label. It is important to bear in mind that if a painting is going to be greatly reduced in size, it must be sufficiently strong and uncomplicated to "read" clearly in the smaller format.

126

LEFT: *This painting was commissioned by HRH Princess Alexandra as a 60th birthday present for her husband, Sir Angus Ogilvy. Their home, Thatched House Lodge, is a building with two very different façades, so I painted both and linked them together using a decorative device. The cartouche incorporates a selection of Sir Angus's pastimes and interests: hunting is represented by a fox and a stag, shooting by a selection of game and literature by a pile of books.*

∘ ∘ ∘

RIGHT: *This Christmas card uses a* chinoiserie *cartouche to frame the words "Peace on Earth", although it could be used to enclose a message for almost any occasion. At the time I worked on this drawing, my studio was full of builders, and peace on earth seemed highly desirable!*

I adapted this cartouche as a cover illustration for the Serenissima Travel brochure, painting the interior of the cartouche as a landscape in full colour set against a black background, the whole having an exotic, jewel-like feeling, quite different from the simpler monochromatic line drawing on this Christmas card.

LEFT: *Sketch of the park side of Thatched House Lodge.*

This cartouche formed the frontispiece for The Fine Art of Dining, *a collection of recipes from world-famous chefs. The cherub in the chef's hat is awakening the baby's sense of taste by dangling a strawberry in front of his mouth. The reclining baby is surrounded by the ingredients of many delicious dinners to come — oysters, lobster, duck, melon, asparagus tips and artichokes. At the top of the cartouche,* putti *revel in the joys of dining in a sylvan glade.*

. . .

I painted Alderley Grange, Gloucestershire, for the owners, Mr and the Hon. Mrs Acloque, in a monochrome of indigo, to give it a moonlit, lyrical, almost dreamy feeling. A cartouche of grisaille with touches of gold leaf reflects both the beauty of the interior and the owners' interest in the arts.

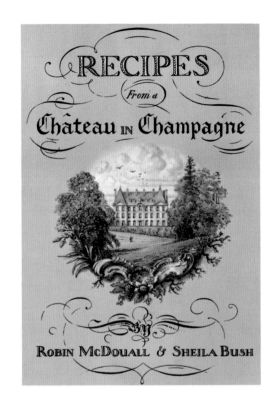

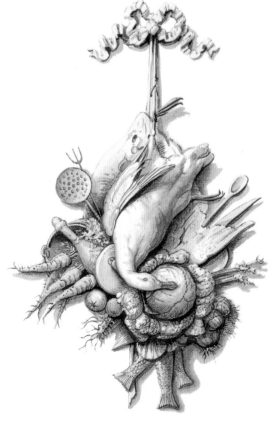

Over the years, I have done quite a lot of work for the champagne company, Moët et Chandon.
This watercolour of the Château de Saran at Epernay was painted for the cover of a book called
Recipes from a Château in Champagne, *featuring the dishes of three chefs. The decoration*
at the base of the vignette includes vines and grapes, and the culinary trophy on the back of the
jacket (RIGHT) *shows a bottle of Dom Perignon with a duck as well as humbler, but no less*
important, ingredients such as a cabbage, carrots and onions. Working at Saran was a great
pleasure — it was always a treat to be greeted at the end of a day's painting by a glass of
champagne — with luck, in the company of Madame de Maigret.

◦ ◦ ◦

This magnificent and unusual Norwegian house, Fritzöehus at Larvik, was painted in grisaille for Herr and Fru Treschow-Stang for reproduction in various different ways. I have taken the family's arms from a nineteenth-century painted room in the house. The branches on either side of it are a symbol of the many splendid trees on the estate.

ABOVE: This painting of Thornton Stud, Yorkshire, was commissioned by Lady Howard de Walden as a present for her husband. As the main house no longer stands, it was decided to paint the very fine entrance gates to the park. I wanted to include a sketch of Lord Howard de Walden's favourite mare with her foal, but it was difficult to represent these two elements as a unified whole within a single painting. I therefore decided to use the device of an open book in trompe l'oeil, *with the two parts of the picture on opposite pages. This particular method can be used as a way of bringing together various aspects of a person's life, work or interests which would not otherwise "fit." Such a painting could be used to commemorate any special anniversary or event where disparate images and information have to be included.*

RIGHT: This painting of the St James's façade of Brooks's Club executed in grisaille, is in a trompe l'oeil *gold frame from plasterwork in the club's card room. Various members of the club, including myself, were asked to contribute to the book* Brooks's: A Social History. *This painting appears on the jacket.*

This view from Arthington Hall was commissioned as a wedding present for its owners, William and Alice Sheepshanks. Arthington is in Yorkshire, and this view, showing the river Wharf, was a subject painted several times by the artist JMW Turner.

I have incorporated various personal elements into this painting as the occasion of the gift made this particularly appropriate. William Sheepshanks proposed to his wife in Seville, so Cupid is seen here shooting his arrow through a Seville orange. The two small side panels show views of Venice, a favourite place, and the tropical fish swimming in the bowl in the foreground are a mutual interest. The grouse feathers, which represent their shoot, have a double meaning: August 12th, the first day of the grouse-shooting season, is also Alice Sheepshanks's birthday. The family crest, a sheep, is in the top panel, and the date of the wedding and the couple's initials are painted on the surrounding ribbon.

Patterns in the Dark

Mary Sheepshanks

LEFT: *The same view, this time by moonlight, was used as a jacket illustration for the poetry book* Patterns in the Dark *by William Sheepshanks's mother, Mary.*

• • •

RIGHT: *This frontispiece, for a cookery book called* Fruits of the Earth, *shows the kitchen garden at Arthington, within a chinoiserie cartouche, which includes the garden's produce and some of the birds that live within its walls.*

The Château de Thoiry near Paris is the home of the Vicomte and Vicomtesse de la Panouse, for whom this was painted. The design in the foreground of the picture is taken from decoration I found on a harpsichord in the château, the work of Christophe Huet, a disciple of Oudry. This design was reproduced on both china and stationery and the original monochrome drawing has been reproduced in black, blue, green and red.

· · ·

BOOKPLATES

· · · · ·

LEFT: A possible alternative to the central image depicted on the bookplate shown below: this more distant view of Ragley, from the west, was painted to commemorate the planting of a new avenue of trees.

· · ·

BELOW: This bookplate shows Ragley Hall, home of the Marquess and Marchioness of Hertford, the Seymour coat of arms and some of Lord Hertford's particular interests. This design has also been used as a postcard and a menu cover.

A bookplate can take many forms but the designs on the following pages incorporate many elements which are personal to their owners. I produce a finished drawing in black and white which can then be printed or, ideally, engraved, although this can be very expensive. A variety of subjects can be represented in the form of a cartouche. For the bookplate shown here (RIGHT), Lady Hertford wanted me to depict her husband's multifarious interests. His love of the theatre is represented by a mask, literature by a book, writing by a quill and parchment, hunting by a riding crop, water-skiing by a mono-ski and farming by a sheaf of corn. His fondness for trees is shown by the oak branches which form the frame on the left, and his time in the army in Egypt by the palms on the right.

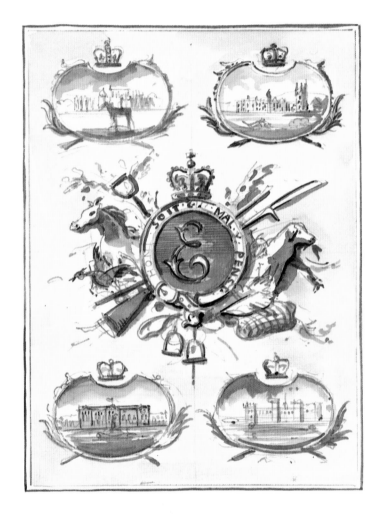

This bookplate for HM the Queen was commissioned as a 60th birthday present by HRH Princess Alexandra and Sir Angus Ogilvy. I submitted these two designs. My idea was to represent Her Majesty's different residences in individual cartouches, with the crown above each roughly corresponding in date. The right-hand sketch includes a centrepiece with elements suggestive of Her Majesty's interests, and the left-hand one shows the royal coat of arms. However, the Princess and Sir Angus finally decided on a version of the design without the four different crowns.

RIGHT: This bookplate, for Fürst and Fürstin zu Ysenburg und Büdingen, depicts Schloss Büdingen and incorporates the Ysenburg arms at the top of the cartouche. This design was also intended for use as a menu cover, and the ribbon has deliberately been left blank so that the appropriate date can be inscribed on it.

• • •

BELOW: This bookplate for Lord King of Wartnaby incorporates his interests of hunting, shooting and fishing. An otter, which is Lord King's crest, is depicted in a naturalistic manner in front of a rural landscape.

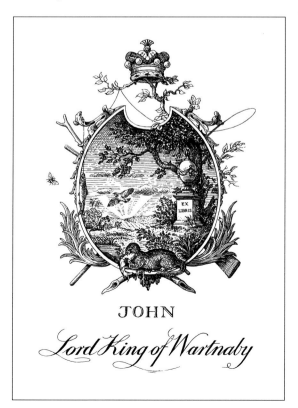

VERITATIS ET ÆQVITATIS BENAX

SOMERTON

Graham Redgrave-Rust

LEFT: I designed this bookplate for myself. My work as a painter is shown by a palette, brushes, mahlstick and portfolio, and my travels by a globe. On the left sits my French bulldog Bella, with a rosa mundi *which represents both love and nature. The palm is symbolic of my Christian faith, and the garland of rosemary and periwinkle beneath the crest represent remembrance and friendship. My house is depicted in the cartouche below. My original designs are usually twice as large as the finished engravings, partly because it is easier to work on a larger scale, and partly because the reduction sharpens the line.*

. . .

RIGHT: If you do not wish to include your house in a bookplate, you may wish to show a landscape which is of particular importance to you, such as this view of a Suffolk village. The plants and flowers depicted in the cartouche were all picked from local hedgerows. I painted the landscape exactly as it appears today, although the sleeping shepherd, whose flock has strayed, is a pastoral convention, harking back to pre-industrial England. Perhaps he is dreaming of England's unmechanised rural past.

ABOVE: A bookplate for Mr Sebastian de Ferranti, incorporating his coat of arms and his various interests and pastimes in a cartouche surrounding a classical landscape.

• • •

LEFT: I painted this juggler bookplate as a present for my godson Geordie Cox, but it could easily be adapted for any child. However, it is worth remembering that you will need one ball for each letter of the child's name — if the planned recipient is a Henrietta or a Marmaduke, the number of balls in the air may test the skill of the juggler!

THE GINGKO TREE

· · · · ·

RIGHT AND BELOW: This design of a gingko tree was commissioned for Baron von Kühlmann by his wife. The idea behind it was that all his friends would contribute to the planting of a grove of gingko trees to mark the occasion of his birthday, and the names of the contributors were to be recorded on the little labels hanging from the tree's branches. However, the number of contributors exceeded our expectations, and extra labels, such as the one shown below, had to be attached to the original tree so that their names could be included, weighing down the slender branches. As a personal touch, I included Baron von Kühlmann's home, Schloss Ramholtz, in the background, together with a centaur to represent his birth sign, Sagittarius. This design could easily be adapted for use as a family tree, with suitably personal symbolism taking the place of the castle and centaur.

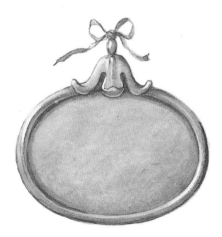

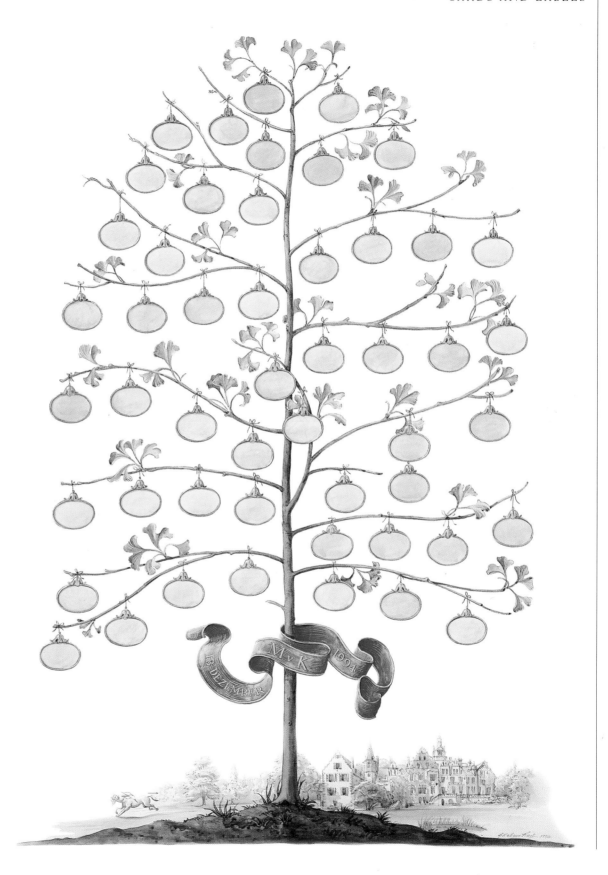

I was commissioned by Lord Howard de Walden to paint his house in Berkshire. I have
included some of the birds — coot, kingfisher, swan and pheasant — that inhabit his estate,
as well as the trout that live in the river. The landscape is painted in a monochrome of
sepia, with a rococo border incorporating an old rose, and a Malmaison carnation in
Lord Howard de Walden's racing colours.

GAME CARD

· · · · ·

HUNGERFORD PARK

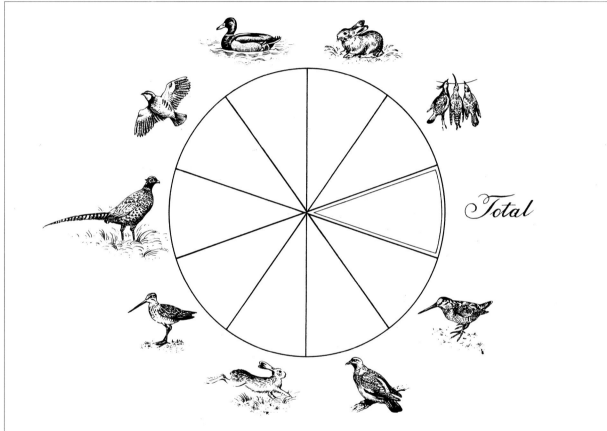

Total

I also designed and painted this game card for Lord Howard de Walden. When closed, the cover of the card shows his crest, surrounded by a box rule executed in his racing colours. Inside, the circle is divided into individual segments, so that the shots can keep a running total of the different game bagged and and tally up the numbers at the end of the day's shoot. Various types of game are shown, including mallard, partridge, pheasant, snipe, hare, wood pigeon, woodcock and rabbit. This idea could easily be adapted for use in other sports: perhaps as a record for an angler or birdwatcher, or as a cricket score card.

146

ABOVE: I was asked to design this menu card for a special birthday party at Claridges for the Hon. Mrs Roland Cubitt. The personal elements here include flowers, shrubs and garden implements to reflect Mrs Cubitt's love of gardening. The open book in the foreground refers to her childhood memoir, An Edwardian Daughter.

MENU CARDS

· · · · ·

When you are producing a limited number of copies of a design, as was the case with the menu card shown on the left, it may be easier, and less expensive, to get them printed as black and white line drawings and then hand-colour them, as I did. The name and date on the drapery can be written in by hand, and the design re-used for another occasion.

ABOVE: This design was commissioned by Lady Elizabeth Anson for her company, Party Planners, as a logo for her stationery and for use as a label on Party Planners' own champagne. Incorporated in the cartouche surrounding the double Ps are elements which reflect the company's work in organising parties and balls and providing good food and wine. The original design, which was executed in black and white, has been reproduced here in red.

ABOVE: The proprietors of Chewton Glen Hotel in the New Forest, Hampshire, asked me to paint the hotel and gardens. In this instance, I produced two identical designs, one a watercolour and the other a line drawing, to be reproduced in a monochrome, as shown in this example in green (RIGHT).

LEFT: This image was used both on the menu, and as a letterhead for the hotel's writing paper.

PANELS AND MURALS

Some walls offer themselves naturally as canvases for murals, but it is not always desirable to paint directly onto a wall — perhaps the space to be filled is an awkward shape or access is difficult. It may simply be more convenient to have a removable panel made to fit the space; a mural is necessarily a permanent feature of a house, whereas a panel can be transported from one house to another, always provided there is a suitable place to display it.

ABOVE: *This landscape, a view of Kingston, Jamaica, from Irishtown, was painted for a specific space. It was originally designed as a removable window panel which formed part of a decorative scheme for a single room. The scene was painted from this sketch (RIGHT), which I made when I was staying as the guest of Brigadier Rupert Green at Up Park Camp in Kingston, home of the Souave bandsmen. I had sketched some of the bandsmen who were so much admired by Queen Victoria, and decided to include the flautist in the painting — a rare treat for me, to be played to as I painted! The lush vegetation of the landscape and brooding sky beautifully offset the musician's splendid uniform.*

THE PARADISE
TRIPTYCH
. . . . .

This triptych, commissioned by Mr and the Hon. Mrs Acloque, was inspired by the work of Hieronymus Bosch. The mahogany panels were salvaged from an old wardrobe, and constructing the triptych was a time-consuming process for the carpenter, Ben Hartley. First he had to fit the panels into the triptych frame, then dis-assemble them for me to paint, and finally re-assemble the whole thing when I had finished, after which the frame was lacquered and gilded by David Cossart. The panels

. . .

LEFT: The outer panels show a globe with a desolate winter landscape. The five members of the Acloque family are shown treading the stony path towards the rising sun on the horizon. I chose these elements to symbolize the struggle of life, sustained by one's hope for, and movement towards, redemption. I have included various Christian symbols in the painting, such as the three crosses, symbolizing the crucifixion of Christ between two thieves, and the scallop shell, representing Christian pilgrimage. The sun and moon are also depicted, and the different configurations of stars show the twelve signs of the Zodiac. The skeleton with the scythe lying beneath the globe represents Death, and the candle beside him is symbolic both of the fleetingness of human life and the hope of life everlasting.

LEFT: This was my first design for the triptych. After a discussion of my clients' requirements, I worked up this design, which, with a few alterations and additions, was transferred, in pencil, onto the virgin gessoed panel.

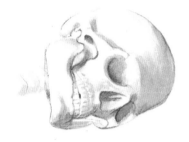

were "gessoed" to prepare them for painting – a process which involves the application of a mixture of chalk and size, after which the panel is sanded down to a glassy smoothness. When this had been completed, I drew the outlines of the design onto the panels in pencil, and painted them first in a monochrome, using watercolour, and then in poly-chrome, in oil.

BELOW AND RIGHT: Studies for the reclining skeleton on the outer panels of the triptych.

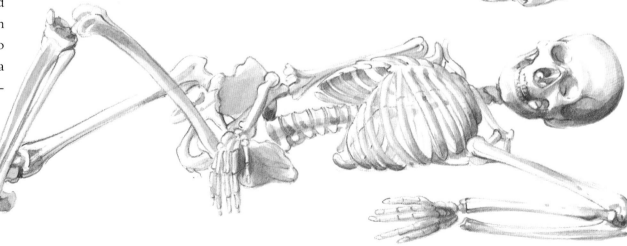

*ABOVE: On the left-hand panel of the triptych, an angel leads a redeemed soul into a paradisical landscape —
a notion reinforced by the inclusion of a bird of Paradise. This panel represents Spring, with seasonal flowers
and birds. The main panel of the triptych has a Summer theme, with appropriate flora and fauna. The lion is
lying down beside the lamb to show that, in Paradise, all will live in harmony. The heavenly city, which I
based on the city of Granada in Spain, is shown at the end of the rainbow, with the dove above it representing
the Holy Ghost; the tree of the knowledge of good and evil stands on the mountain. In the autumnal panel, on
the right-hand side, the watchful, predatory fox is a reminder that the harmony of Paradise can be disrupted.
The goats signify lust and sin, and the dragon is symbolic of the Devil.*

ARMORIAL TROPHIES

o o o o o

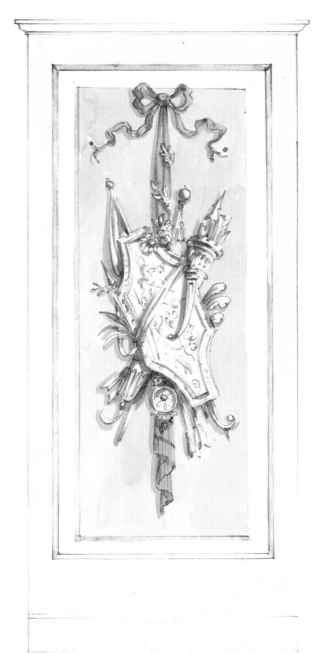

These two armorial trophies (LEFT AND RIGHT) were painted onto separate panels to be positioned above a fireplace (BELOW) in a neo-Palladian house in Frankfurt. The high, galleried room features a painting on the barrel-vaulted ceiling showing the Greek goddess Aurora bringing the dawn, and the martial subject-matter above the fireplace echoed other decoration in the room. My sources for the different pieces of weaponry were plasterwork designs and engravings.

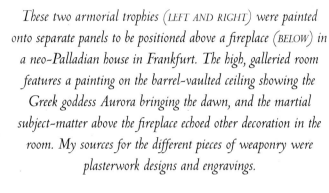

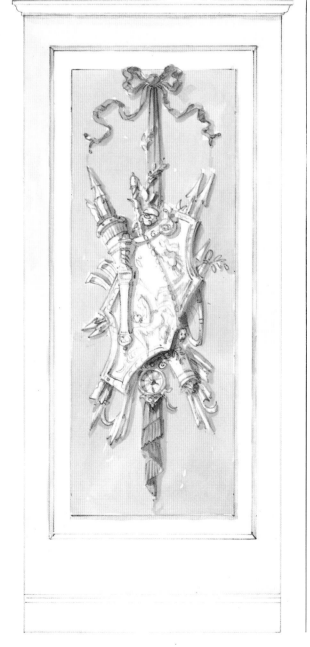

THE CABBAGE THEME

· · · · ·

154

For drawing purposes, the cabbage is one of my favourite vegetables. It has an interesting texture, a beautiful shape and a strong, sculptural form, rather like a fleshier and more substantial rose. Moreover, unlike roses, cabbages are hardy and don't tend to wilt while you are trying to paint them, which is an enormous advantage. The cabbage and the other elements in these paintings are taken from various studies of vegetables and other plants that I have made over the years.

RIGHT: Here, the cabbage has become a magic cabbage in a moonlit landscape, surrounded by creatures of the night such as bats, moths, an owl and a mole. The bewitched youth leans against the stalk waiting for the dawn. This study is in grisaille.

· · ·

BELOW: A study of a marrow plant with a detail of the flower.

RIGHT: Although the shape of the cabbage suggested a roundel, I decided on an octagonal panel. In this particular instance, I did not want to paint directly onto the wood, so I glued some canvas onto the panel and painted on that. Canvas can add more texture to a painting, especially if a smooth finish is not desirable. The extra "dimension" given by the weave of the canvas can also be very attractive. It is worth remembering that some canvases are finer than others, and it is possible to prime a canvas to such an extent that you lose the weave almost entirely. If you are painting on a panel that is neither square nor rectangular, it is far easier to have the required shape cut out of a board and to glue your canvas straight onto it, rather than trying to create an elaborate, many-sided stretcher for the canvas. This particular panel is 60 inches in diameter.

· · ·

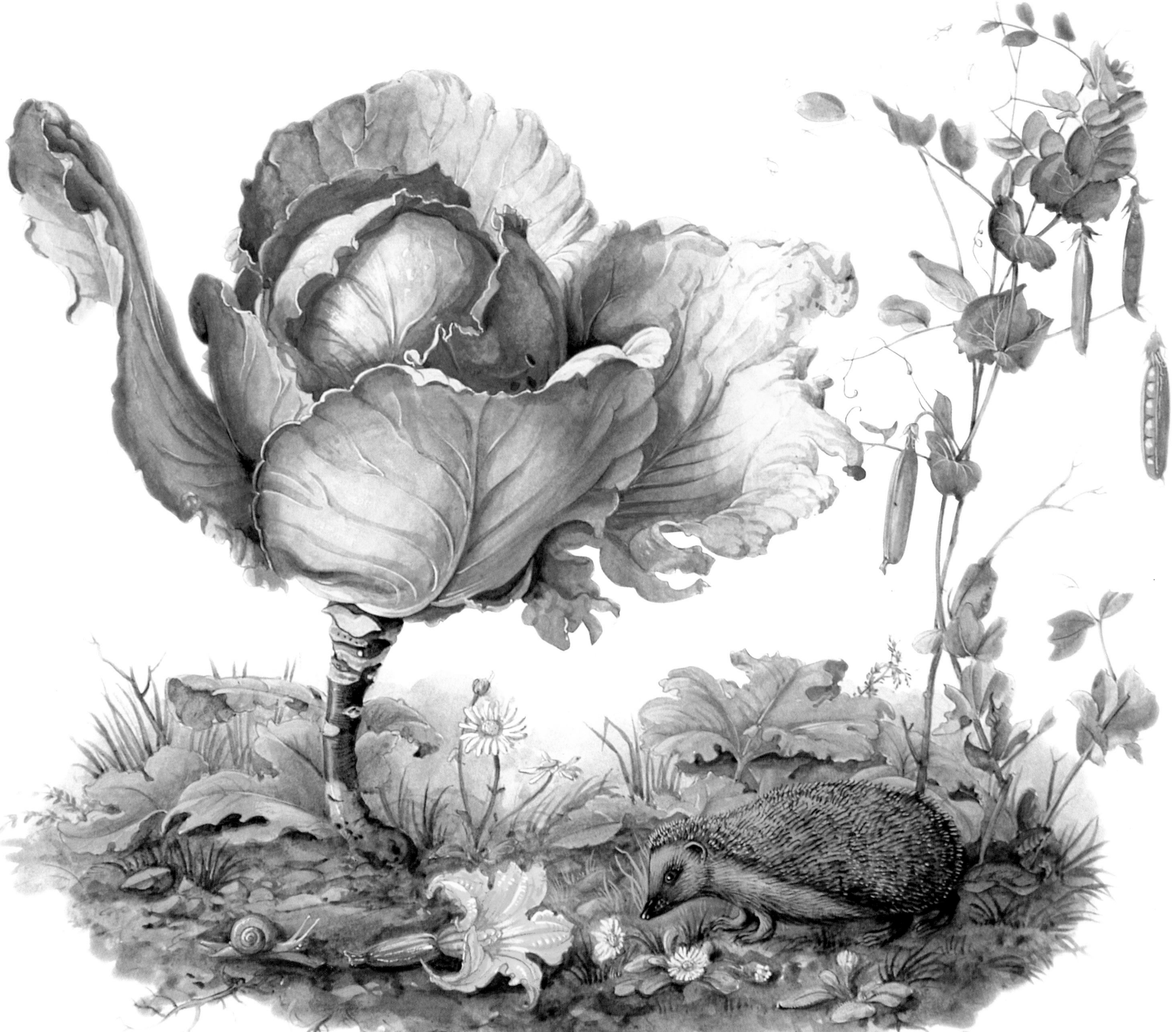

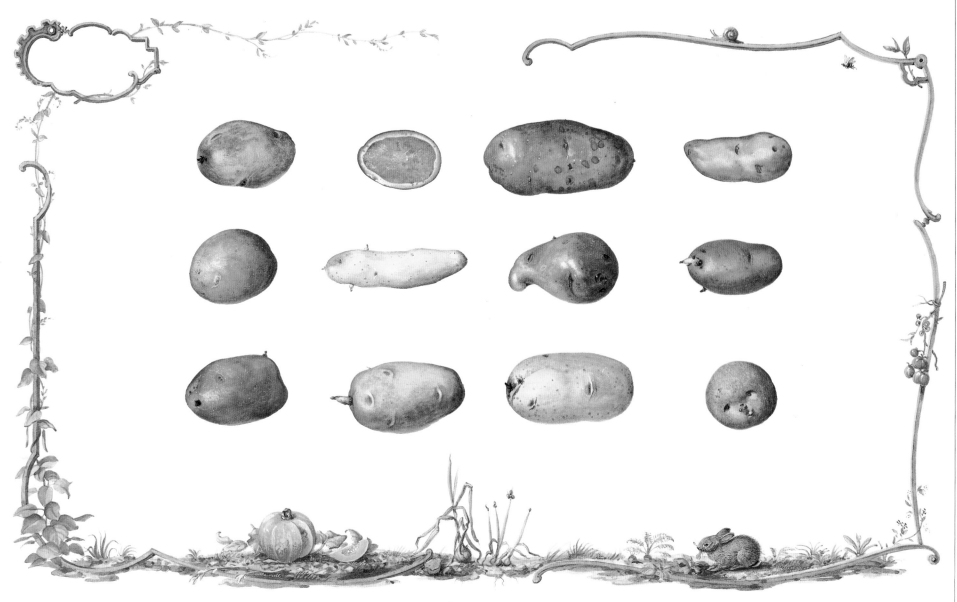

LEFT: *The cabbage is repeated here, with a hedgehog, surrounded by peas, courgettes and flowers.*

RIGHT: *These Welsh onions were one of several studies I made in the kitchen garden at Arthington in Yorkshire (see page 135).*

ABOVE: *This cartouche is one of four, representing the seasons of the year. Autumn is shown here, with the fruits of the harvest: a pumpkin, onions, beans and tomatoes. Four such panels could be painted for a kitchen, with seasonal central motifs such as game, fish, fruits, nuts or vegetables, as illustrated here by these different varieties of potato.*

MAGIC CABBAGE PANEL

. . . . .

The boy in the painting opposite is taking a moonlight ride, not on a carpet, but on a leaf from the magic cabbage *(see page 154)*. A Russian townscape, with the onion-like domes of St Basil's Cathedral, stretches out beneath him as he flies through the night. This "flying cabbage leaf" idea could be developed into a series of picture stories about a child who sets off on a magic cabbage leaf every night for a different adventure — as he travels, he clutches the edge of the leaf and peers over at the various landscapes unfolding below him. This would give ample opportunity for a number of contrasting panels showing exotic landscapes, either real or imagined: in addition to this Russian scene, a scene of Bedouin tents in the desert, a Chinese landscape with pagodas, and a tropical rain forest with lush greenery, would provide plenty of scope for any artist.

ABOVE: I completed several studies of cabbage leaves before selecting one for the panel opposite.

ABOVE: This design could be painted on a panel for a child's bedroom or nursery. Children's tastes change as they grow up, and as their bedroom walls tend to reflect this, painted panels may be preferable to a permanent feature such as a mural. When the child feels that he or she has outgrown this form of decoration, the panel can always be passed on to a younger sibling. Children often like to touch paintings, as well as looking at them, so it is a good idea to use waterproof paints which can easily be wiped clean of sticky finger marks and scribbled additions.

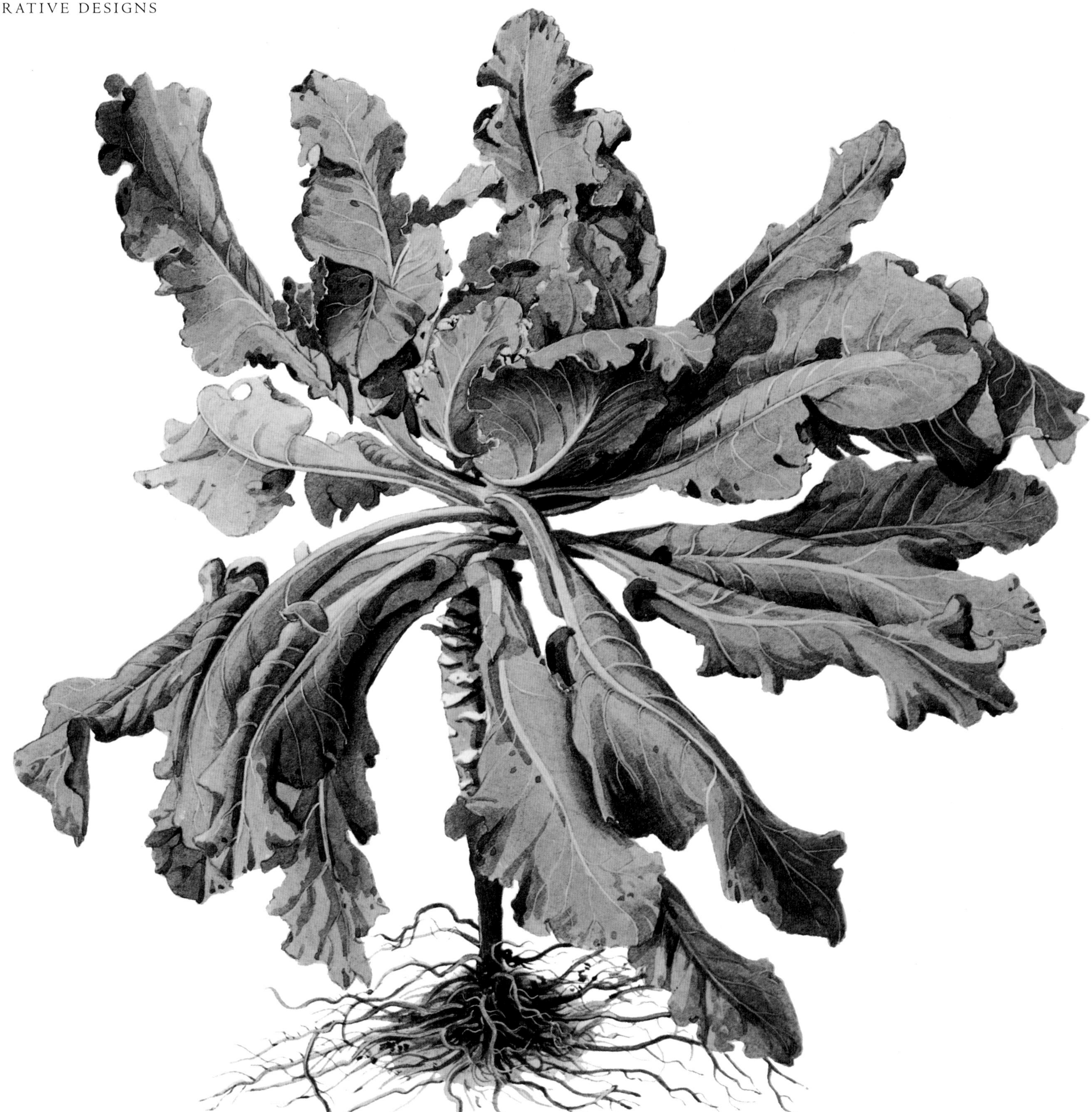

CAULIFLOWER
WINDOW PANEL

· · · ·

BELOW: I designed this panel as a removable shutter for a circular window, because the shape was not sympathetic to a blind or curtain. When the panel is in place, the effect is such that it looks as though a cauliflower in a terracotta pot is standing on the window ledge. It was painted by Rui Paes to my design.

· · ·

LEFT: One of my watercolour studies of the cauliflower plant.

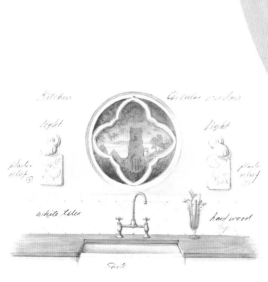

PYRAMIDS OF FLOWERS

. . . . .

Over the years, I have made many studies of individual flowers, and these large decorative pieces are the perfect means of displaying them all together in a way that could never happen in nature. A bay tree forms the structural part of the pyramid, and I have painted in the different flowers so that they look as if they were somehow attached to it.

To create the illusion that the pyramid of flowers is actually standing on a piece of furniture in the room, you could paint in an appropriate support such as the bracket *(shown below left)* or a niche *(below right)*, depending on the architecture and design of the room. Two of these floral pyramids could be used to great effect on either side of French windows, or to brighten up an alcove or a dark room where real flowers and plants will not thrive, such as an entrance hall without daylight.

I have taken a multi-coloured theme and ignored the seasons, but flowers of a single colour or season would be equally effective.

. . .

A variation of these particular flower pyramids is used in the Venus and Mars in Arcadia *mural on page 177. Isolating a portion of a mural and reproducing it on a separate panel can be very successful, provided that the image chosen is strong enough to be removed from its context.*

POUSSIN PANELS

· · · · ·

H ere, I have taken three works by the French artist Nicholas Poussin and reproduced them on panels with different *trompe l'oeil* plasterwork frames. These paintings are favourites of mine, but works by any other artist might be chosen for this purpose. I chose these because their colour schemes worked well in the green and white panelled room in which they were painted. It was also important that they complemented the existing seventeenth-century painting hanging in the room. Poussin's paintings are rectangular in shape, and my *trompe l'oeil* frames are not, so I have to adapted the compositions in order to fit.

· · ·

The painting on the left-hand side is The Nurture of Jupiter, *showing the baby god being fed by the goat Amalthea on the slopes of Mount Ida. The central panel contains the painting* Midas Giving Thanks to Bacchus *in which King Midas is thanking the god Bacchus for granting his wish that everything he touches may turn to gold. The third painting, on the right-hand side, is* The Dance to the Music of Time, *an allegorical piece showing four figures dancing to music played by the figure of Time on a lyre. The figures represent four human experiences: Poverty, Riches, Work and Pleasure. Above the dancers, the god Apollo drives across the sky in his chariot, accompanied by personifications of the Seasons.*

THE LANCERS

· · · · ·

This painting was commissioned by the 16th 5th Regiment of Lancers to commemorate HM The Queen's presentation of a new guidon (small flag) to the regiment, an event which takes place once every 25 years. In order to depict the ceremony and include the various displays and activities of the regiment on the day, I decided to create a painting in the form of a series of panels, based on a design for plasterwork by Robert Adam.

One of the constraints of this sort of commission is that there is little room for the artist's interpretation: in order to include all the necessary soldiers and dignitaries in the composition, the figures had to be drawn on a fairly small scale, and as parade grounds are flat and featureless, there was a risk that the whole thing would look barren. The other problem I had to contend with is that soldiers standing to attention *en masse* make a rigid shape, and it was difficult to invest the painting with any sense of movement or flow. However, the combination of several differently-shaped paintings within a single frame helped to give the painting some movement, and to incorporate scenes of differing proportion, such as the long lines of soldiers and tanks.

Studies of the Queen's hat, handbag and dress. On the day of the parade, I did as many sketches as I could and took plenty of photographs, but a great deal of activity was happening at some distance away and I was not able to note as much detail as I would have wished. Consequently, I later visited Buckingham Palace where the Queen's dresser produced the clothes that Her Majesty had been wearing on the day of the ceremony and I was allowed to make some additional studies of them for use in the painting.

ABOVE: The finished painting, which now hangs in the officers' mess at the home of the regiment in Tidworth, Hampshire.

166

FLOWER SERIES

· · · · ·

Flower studies can be used in many different ways *(see also page 162)*. The studies of different flowers on the following pages could form the basis for either a series of panels or a set of roller blinds. Irises, with their exquisite shapes and velvety texture, are always a pleasure to paint. I have also painted daffodils and pheasant's eye narcissi as part of this series *(see page 170)*. All of the irises were

ABOVE: Iris blind design.

· · ·

LEFT: Spartan iris study.

ABOVE AND RIGHT: Ringo iris detail and study.

obtained from Kellway's Nursery in Somerset.

I have adopted the format of a rococo cartouche at the base of each plant, with a space for recording its name. I have included a variety of small creatures and insects, such as the bee and ladybird on the Spartan iris (*LEFT*) and the bee and the vole on the Ringo iris (*RIGHT*), to give some additional interest.

Iris stems are often very long and the effect, from an artist's point of view, can sometimes seem too "leggy." In order to create the proportions needed for the study, I have employed the device, sometimes used in botanical drawing, of "cutting" the stem. The mark on the stem clearly indicates that a portion has been removed.

If you decide to create a series of roller blinds rather than panels, it is worth remembering that, in

order to avoid painting large flat areas of colour, you can pre-order a blind of your desired background colour. Make sure that the blind has a reasonably smooth texture, as this will make painting easier – a holland material is preferable to something with a pronounced weave in it. When working on the image, apply the paint thinly, so that it will not crack when you roll up the blind.

· · ·

LEFT AND ABOVE: Iris studies. It is often helpful to make studies of individual parts of a plant, such as leaves and petals, before beginning your final composition.

ABOVE: *A design for one of a pair of iris panels, using one yellow and one white bearded iris in urns, surrounded by songbirds and insects in a* trompe l'oeil *alcove with rococo decoration. You could employ this design as the basis for a series of panels showing different specimen plants, depending on the size and proportions of the space you wish to decorate. The urn here is painted as if in stone — a variation on this could be terracotta or perhaps blue and white delftware. For an extension of the* trompe l'oeil *effect, the "alcove" could be painted in the same colour as the walls of the room. These were painted on stretched canvas, but they could easily be painted directly on the wall itself.*

LEFT: *Studies of a bearded iris plant and petals.*

ABOVE: If you are painting a series of panels, it may be necessary to balance the weight of a single bloom in one panel with several blooms in the next. Here are two different angles of narcissi.

. . .

RIGHT: Painting of narcissi. Although I have chosen to paint a single botanical study on each individual blind, posies or garlands of cut flowers would make equally strong images, perhaps representing the seasons.

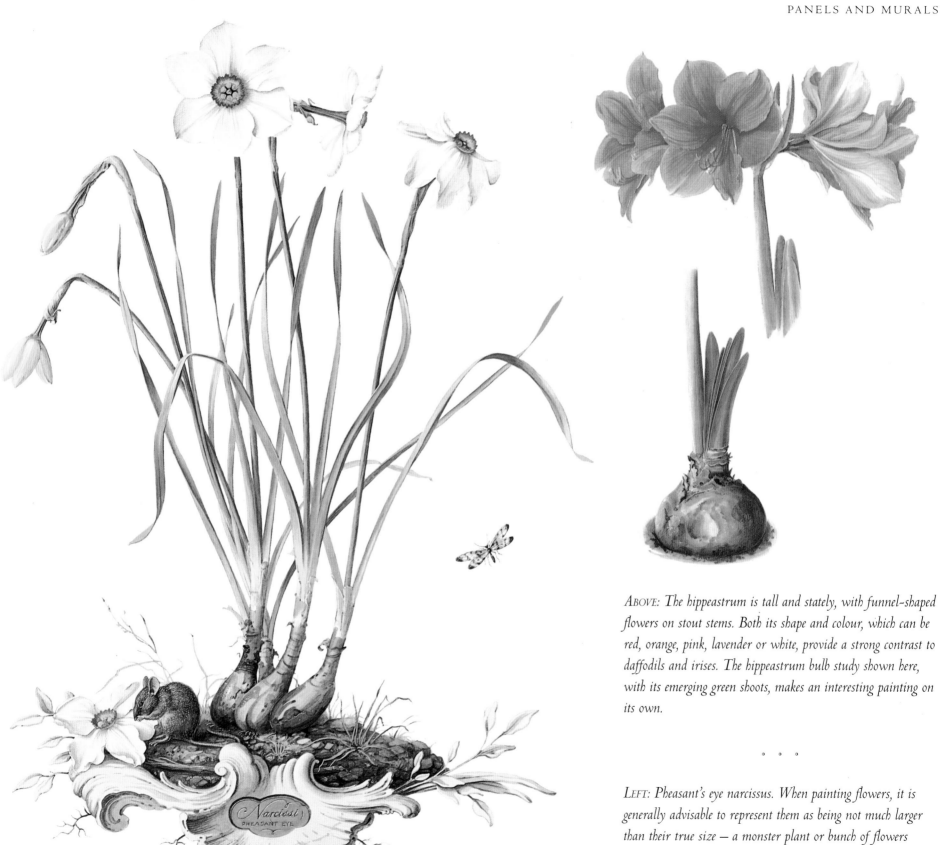

ABOVE: The hippeastrum is tall and stately, with funnel-shaped flowers on stout stems. Both its shape and colour, which can be red, orange, pink, lavender or white, provide a strong contrast to daffodils and irises. The hippeastrum bulb study shown here, with its emerging green shoots, makes an interesting painting on its own.

LEFT: Pheasant's eye narcissus. When painting flowers, it is generally advisable to represent them as being not much larger than their true size — a monster plant or bunch of flowers usually succeeds in looking bizarre rather than attractive!

THE PAINTED STAIRCASE

. . . . .

This staircase was commissioned by Fürst and Fürstin Zu Ysenburg und Büdingen for a pavilion in the grounds of their home, Schloss Büdingen. The designs are based on the tales collected by the brothers Jakob and Wilhelm Grimm, who lived a few miles away. Stories which particularly appealed to the Fürstin were chosen to be represented in a series of different panels, some of which are shown here. In order to unify the representations of the various tales, I divided up the available space architecturally into panels, and surrounded each painting with *trompe l'oeil* plasterwork in pale earth colours.

I found that some tales lent themselves to illustration more easily than others. Some stories, such as *Rapunzel*, contain one very compelling visual image — the girl in the tower letting down her long plait of hair for the Prince to climb — which simply demands to be painted; others do not, and it was difficult to know what to choose.

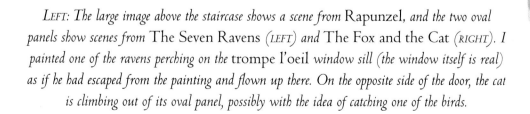

LEFT: The large image above the staircase shows a scene from Rapunzel, *and the two oval panels show scenes from* The Seven Ravens *(LEFT) and* The Fox and the Cat *(RIGHT). I painted one of the ravens perching on the* trompe l'oeil *window sill (the window itself is real) as if he had escaped from the painting and flown up there. On the opposite side of the door, the cat is climbing out of its oval panel, possibly with the idea of catching one of the birds.*

. . .

RIGHT: This panel shows a scene from The Elves and the Shoemaker.

ABOVE: *The two oval panels on either side of the window show scenes from* The Golden Bird (LEFT) *and* The Devil with the Three Golden Hairs (RIGHT).

• • •

RIGHT: *Two large rectangular panels on the left-hand side of the draped doorway show scenes from* The Valiant Little Tailor, *and the panel on the right-hand side a scene from* The Frog King.

LEFT: The scene shown in the left-hand panel is taken from The Spirit in the Bottle. *To the right of the draped door are two scenes from* The Golden Bird.

BELOW: The two irregularly shaped staircase panels show scenes from the stories The Blue Light *(LEFT) and* Frau Holle *(RIGHT).*

Illustrations of fairy tales would make an excellent decoration for a child's bedroom — however, the subject matter of some of the Grimm Brothers' tales is rather frightening, and it would be wise to steer clear of anything that might give the child nightmares!

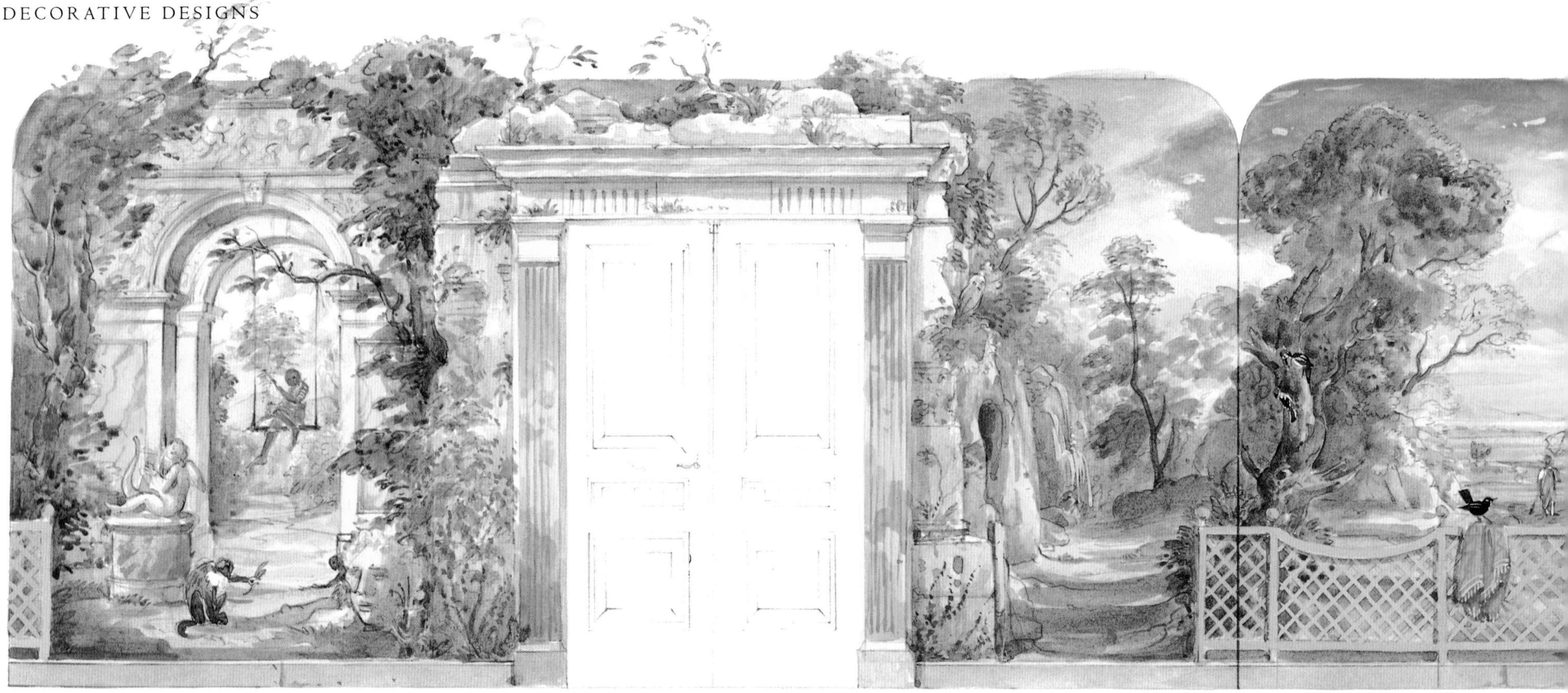

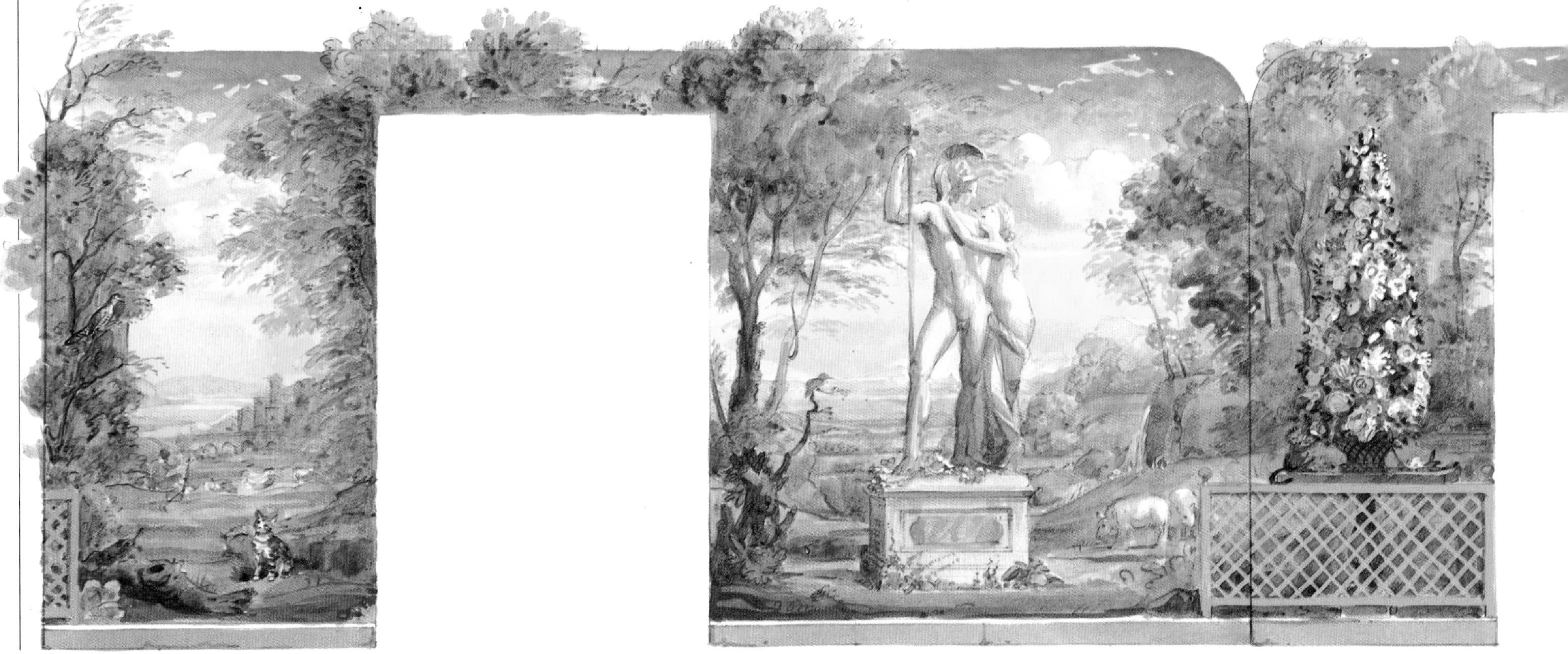

MARS AND VENUS IN ARCADIA

· · · · ·

I was asked to create a mural to cover all four walls and the ceiling of the dining room in a house in Frankfurt, and to design a mosaic marble floor. The Arcadian landscape centres around a statue of Mars and Venus embracing, by the Italian sculptor Antonio Canova. Rui Paes assisted me with this project and was responsible for painting the birds and animals.

I painted the ceiling as a continuation of the sky, and added some passing clouds and a few birds. As this room does not have a very high ceiling, anything more elaborate would have had the effect of lowering it and possibly making those dining feel rather oppressed.

Where pieces of furniture stand against the wall, I painted the panels with a trellis pattern – after all, there is little point in labouring over details if they will be obscured! The floral pyramids have been painted to create a *trompe l'oeil* effect, as though they are in the room rather than part of the landscape *(see page 162)*.

ABOVE: *The mosaic floor of the room, designed by me, in conjunction with Rui Paes, incorporates the moon and the stars.*

CASTLE RISING

· · · · ·

These panels were commissioned by Mr and Mrs Greville Howard, who live at Castle Rising in Norfolk. The armorial trophy (*BELOW*) was designed as an overdoor panel for double doors leading off the hall, and, to keep it in harmony with the existing decoration, it was executed in a monochrome of umber with some gilding.

The original design (LEFT) was felt to be too rococo in feeling, and the neo-classical trophy (ABOVE) was preferred.

· · ·

RIGHT: This small oval panel, also an overdoor, shows Diana the huntress pursuing a stag in a wooded landscape. The subject was felt to be appropriate as Mrs Howard enjoys hunting. The panel was painted in grisaille, with the only colour being provided by the feathers tied with a green ribbon to a pin — a keepsake perhaps, from a hunting expedition — which have been attached to the painting.

180

NEWFIELD

∘ ∘ ∘ ∘ ∘

Newfield was designed and built some years ago in the Palladian style by the architect Quinlan Terry for Mr and Mrs Michael Abrahams. The owners' intention was to decorate the central hall with murals, and the theme for the landscape within the painted architectural framework was designed to incorporate both their own interests and several of the most noteworthy local landmarks.

Newfield is situated in North Yorkshire, near the magnificent park and gardens of Studley Royal, which contain not only the splendid ruins of the 12th-century Cistercian Fountains Abbey but also several exquisite 18th-century pavilions and temples. I have included some of them, such as the Temple of Piety shown opposite, in the mural.

∘ ∘ ∘

OPPOSITE: Mr Abrahams was a Master of Foxhounds, so cubs with a hunting horn and riding crop are at play around the base of one of the two large urns which I painted in the spaces between the windows. The Prince of Wales's feathers are painted on this urn to record a visit made by Prince Charles to Newfield while the mural was in progress. Various local birds are represented on the second urn, including an Arctic tern and a pheasant.

ABOVE: The monkey and the rich draperies and tassels give a theatrical, Venetian atmosphere to this landscape, which is very much in keeping with the architectural style of the house.

ABOVE: My intention in this portrait was to suggest that the Palladian spirit was brought to Yorkshire from Venice, and is here represented as being released from a gilded birdcage in the form of the Villa Rotonda.

ACKNOWLEDGEMENTS

∘ ∘ ∘ ∘ ∘

182

The author and publishers would like to thank the following people for allowing work from their collections to be reproduced in this book:

H.M. The Queen: Page 69 (bottom left)

H.M. The Queen of the Belgians: Page 41 (bottom)

H.M. King Hussein bin Talal G.C.B., G.C.V.O. Page 73 (top left)

Mr and Mrs Michael Abrahams: Page 180, 181

Mr and the Hon. Mrs Acloque: Pages 129, 141, 149 (top), 150, 151 (top), 152

The Duke and Duchess of Argyll: Page 67 (bottom right)

The Lady Ashcombe: Page 68 (right)

Philip Astley-Jones Esq.: Page 154 (right)

The Lady Astor of Hever: Page 69 (top right)

Stephen Bales, Esq.: Pages 65, 78, 115, 128, 166 (left), 167 (right)

Miss Beverley Battersby: Page 171 (left)

Mrs Jane Bell: Page 171 (bottom right)

Mr and Mrs Roy Bostock: Page 170 (right)

Miss Rosemary Carey: Page 81 (bottom)

Mrs de Bianchi Cossart: Page 154 (left)

David Cossart, Esq.: Pages 41 (top), 58 (right), 70, 114 (left), 133

Master Geordie Cox: Page 142 (left)

Albert Cummings, Esq.: Page 31

Mrs Felicity Dahl: Page 74 (left)

The Duke and Duchess of Devonshire: Page 66 (right)

Gunilla Gräfin Douglas: Page 111 (top)

Graf Douglas Langenstein: Pages 62, 76 (left), 77 (right)

The Lord and Lady Eden: Page 124 (bottom left)

Michael Elles, Esq.: Page 12

Sebastian de Ferranti Esq.: Page 142 (right)

Gainsborough's House, Sudbury: Page 72

Mr and Mrs Chandos Gore Langton: Pages 1, 80

Monsieur Gui Weill Goudchaux: Page 85 (top)

The Vicountess Hambleden: Page 171 (top right)

The Earl and Countess of Harewood: Page 67 (top right)

Mr and Mrs Martyn Hedley: Pages 24 (top left), 125

The Marquess of Hertford: Page 137 (right)

Mr and Mrs Greville Howard: Page 178, 179

The Lady King of Wartnaby: Page 120

The Lord King of Wartnaby: Page 139 (left)

Mr and Mrs James Kirkman: Page 30

The Baron von Kühlmann: Page 143

The 16th 5th Lancers: Page 165

The Duke and Duchess of Marlborough: Page 69 (top centre)

Môet et Chandon (London) Ltd: Page 130

The National Trust: Page 69 (bottom right)

The Duke and Duchess of Norfolk: Page 66 (left)

The Duke and Duchess of Northumberland: Page 69 (top left)

The Hon. Sir Angus Ogilvy: Page 126

Señhor Rui Andrade Paes: Pages 45, 157 (top centre)

The Vicomte and Vicomtesse de la Panouse: Page 136

Mrs C. Pilkington: Page 169 (left)

Mr and Mrs Alistair Robertson: Pages 60, 61

The Marquess and Marchioness of Salisbury: Page 67 (top left)

Martin Skan Esq.: Page 147

Lady Elizabeth Shakerley: Page 146 (right)

Major B.M.H. Shand M.C., D.L.: Page 146 (left)

Mrs Mary Sheepshanks: Pages 113 (top), 135

Mr and Mrs William Sheepshanks: Page 134

The Earl and Countess of Shelburne: Page 67 (bottom left)

Herr and Fru Treschow-Stang: Page 131

The Lord and Lady Howard de Walden: Pages 132, 144, 145

Mrs J. Walmsley: Page 85 (bottom)

Collection of The Earl of Yarmouth: Page 137 (left)

The Earl and Countess of Yarmouth: Page 54

Fürst and Fürstin zu Ysenburg und Büdingen: Pages 139 (right), 172-174

The Artist: Cover, pages 4, 7, 8, 9-11, 15, 16, 18-29, 31, 33-36, 38-40, 42-44, 46-53, 56, 57, 58 (left), 59, 63, 64, 68 (left), 73 (bottom left and right), 75, 76 (right), 77 (top left), 79, 81 (top), 82-84, 86-103, 106-110, 111(bottom), 112, 113 (bottom), 114 (right), 116-119, 121-123, 124 (right), 127, 138, 140, 148, 149 (bottom), 151 (bottom), 156, 157 (top), 158, 159, 161, 162, 164, 166 (right), 167 (left), 168, 169 (right), endpapers

Private Collections: Pages 3, 71, 74 (right), 104, 105, 153, 155, 157 (bottom), 160, 163, 170 (left), 177

Endpapers: Sonnet by Michelangelo Buonarroti

I' mi son caro assai più ch'i' non solio;
poi ch'i' t'ebbi nel cor più di me vaglio,
come pietra c'aggiuntovi l'intaglio
è di più pregio che 'l suo primo scolio.

O come scritta o pinta carta o foglio
più si riguarda d'ogni straccio o taglio,
tal di me fo, da po' ch'i' fu' berzaglio
segnato dal tuo viso, e non mi doglio.

Sicur con tale stampa in ogni loco
vo, come quel c'ha incanti o arme seco,
c'ogni periglio gli fan venir meno

I' vaglio contr'a l'acqua e contr'al foco,
col segno tuo rallumino ogni cieco
e col mi sputo sano ogni veleno.